MARCO VAN DUYVENDIJK
PORTRAITS FROM ASIA

MARCO VAN DUYVENDIJK
PORTRAITS FROM ASIA

DANIEL STRONG, CURATOR

WITH INTRODUCTION AND COMMENTARY BY
MARCO VAN DUYVENDIJK

FAULCONER GALLERY, GRINNELL COLLEGE
2006

FOREWORD

This catalogue was published on the occasion of Marco van Duyvendijk's first museum exhibition outside of his native Holland and the first to include photographs from each of the four Asian countries he has visited: China, Mongolia, Taiwan, and South Korea. I first saw his photographs at the booth of his gallery—Galerie Cokkie Snoei, Rotterdam—at Paris Photo 2005, and approached him that same day about developing an exhibition. He had not yet been to Taiwan or South Korea. The exhibition and catalogue have evolved along with his work, a sign of the commitment the Faulconer Gallery makes to the artists it presents.

A self-taught photographer, van Duyvendijk brings a background in psychology to bear in his portraits of people he meets on his travels. By approaching strangers with no prior arrangement and asking them to pose, he employs the method of a documentary photographer while turning the typical request of a tourist on its head: instead of asking strangers to take his picture, he asks strangers for permission to take theirs. Upon doing so he takes his subject's name and address and repays the courtesy with a print of the finished work.

During an exhibition in Holland of portraits he had made during a stay in Romania, he was invited by the consul from the Mongolian consulate to spend two seasons in Mongolia—winter 2003 and summer 2004—and photograph whatever he pleased. Many of the photographs resulting from those two trips are included here. He traveled to China in 2005, Taiwan in spring 2006, and South Korea in summer 2006.

While his subjects from Mongolia and China vary widely, he approached South Korea and Taiwan with particular subjects in mind. His series from these two countries focus on women at different stages of their lives: at school and at work. As in all of his work, he presents these experiences as distinct from each other as they are distinct from his own.

Since the decline of empire, or at least its reputation's decline, the practice of westerners venturing abroad to "represent" other cultures has become suspect, to say the least. No attempt has been made by van Duyvendijk to represent the whole of Mongolian, Chinese, Taiwanese, and South Korean culture in his photographs. He freely, and wisely, admits that his work represents his own interests and desires, not those of his subjects.

But in the days when virtually all words to describe a photographer's project are charged, what is the photographer to shoot, and furthermore, what is the curator to say? As a curator, I am as uncomfortable with the charge of "representing" Marco's photographs in words as he is of the charge of "representing" an entire culture in a photograph of a Mongolian nomad or a Taiwanese nut seller. The task of effectively—or not so effectively—translating an artist's visual language into a verbal/literary language has never been my fondest part of the job. Fortunately, Marco's photographs need few words of explanation to reveal their power.

Representation, "other", desire, power—these words can be found batted back and forth among cultural theorists in scores of books and blogs easily found on the Internet. This book is not about words, but pictures. See for yourself.

DANIEL STRONG

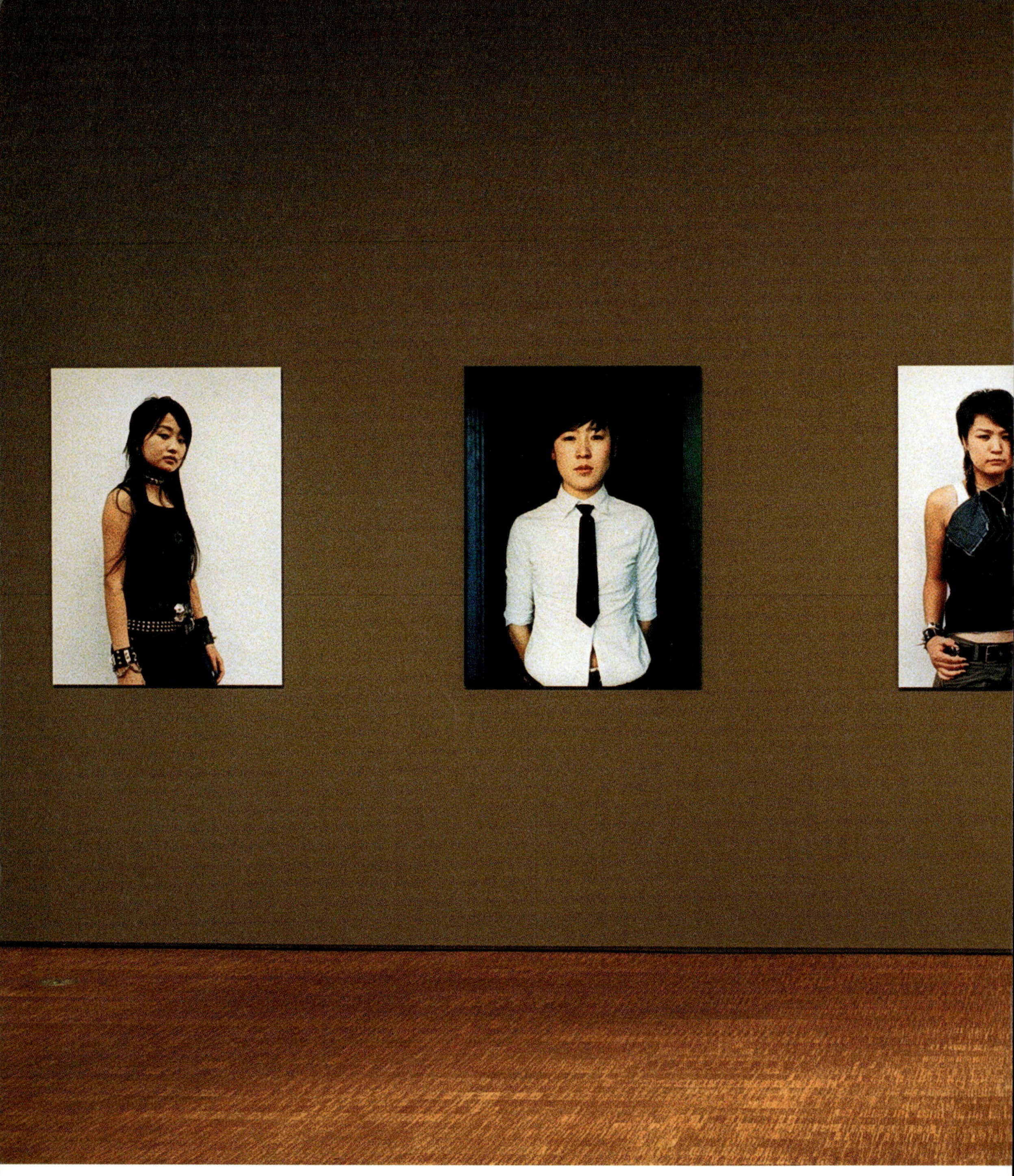

Installation view, Faulconer Gallery

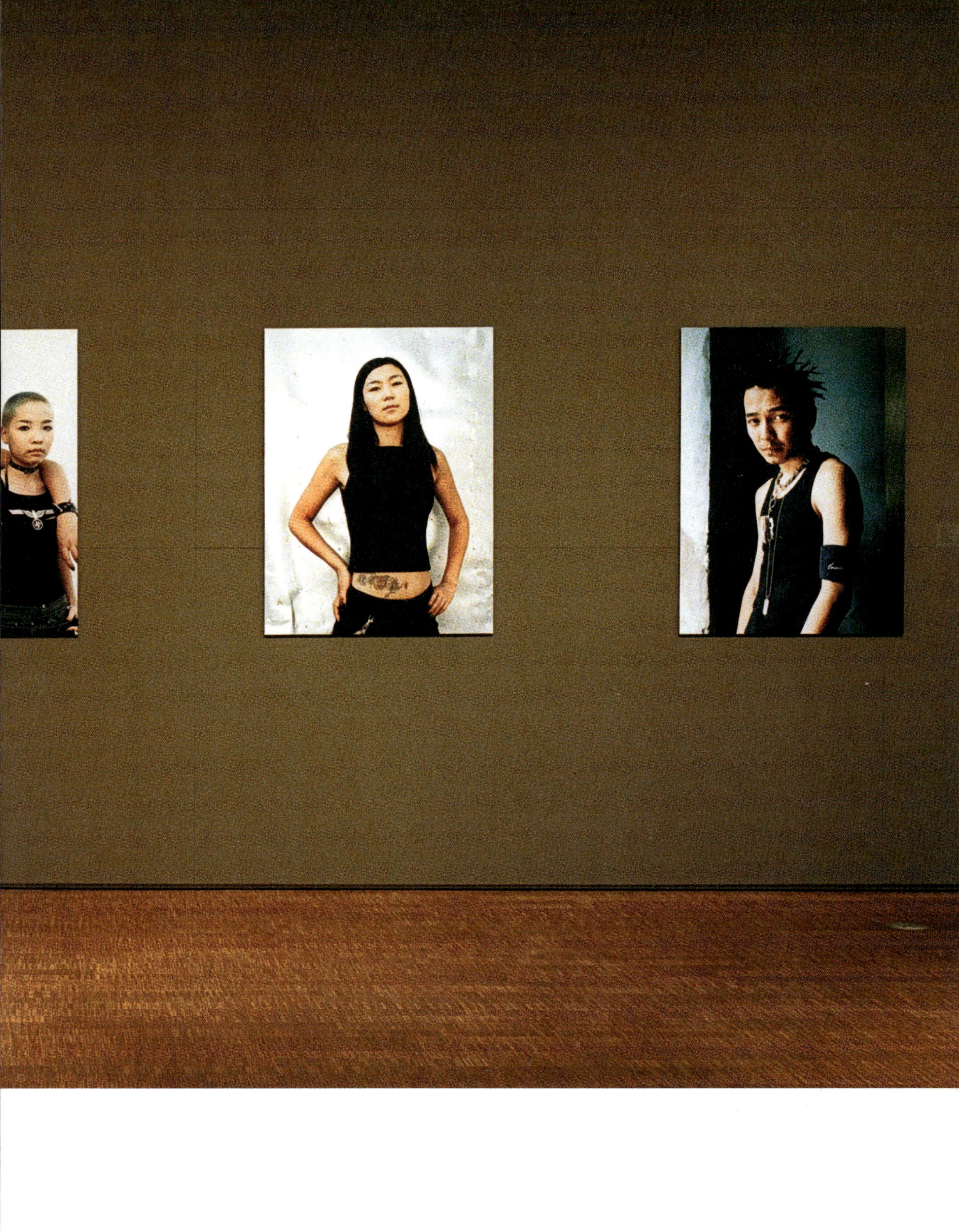

INTRODUCTION

In summer of 2003 I met Jan Brummelhuis, then the consul of Mongolia to the Netherlands, who had seen my exhibition of Eastern European photographs at Huis Marseille, a museum for photography in Amsterdam. He suggested it was time for someone to make a good photographic series about Mongolia. I did my best to persuade him that I was the photographer to do it. Several months later, in early winter, I made my first trip to Asia. After having the opportunity to spend one winter and summer in Mongolia, I found new projects, first in China in 2005, then Taiwan and South Korea in 2006.

In Mongolia I had the chance to explore a large part of the country, while in China I remained for the most part in the city of Guangzhou. In Taiwan I concentrated only on the fascinating culture of the Betel Nut Beauties, while in South Korea I found myself sitting at the school desk again. The photos in this book show elements of all these countries, sometimes in an obvious way, sometimes unexpected, but they are mere pinpoints in this large and diverse continent. Even if I wanted to, it would be impossible to give a complete image of a country. My desire to make my own artistic and personal decisions is greater than my desire to be objective or comprehensive.

When working in Asia I always work with a translator. Without a translator most of the pictures would not have been possible. I am very much indebted to my translators, who shared great friendship and good humor, open-mindedness and patience during my visits to their countries. I would like to thank Altantsetseg and Uyanga in Mongolia, Ma Ling in China, Ingrid in Taiwan and Sun-Hee Kim in South Korea for the help they gave me. In addition to my translators, I received assistance from Evert Groenendijk; the staff at the Consulate of the Netherlands in Guangzhou, China; staff at the Artist Village in Taipei, Taiwan; and from Sejin Kim in Seoul, South Korea.

Back home in the Netherlands I am grateful to Gerrit-Jan van Ek and the photography staff at the newspaper, De Volkskrant. Many of the pictures in this book were previously published in the newspaper and the trip to South Korea would not have happened without it. Thanks to my gallerist in

Rotterdam, Cokkie Snoei, for promoting my work.
Thanks to Sabine for understanding that
sometimes I just have to go and explore the world.

In Iowa I would like to thank Milton Severe,
exhibition designer at the Faulconer Gallery, and
Annabel Wimer, designer of this book, for their
sensitive and beautiful presentation of my work. I
also thank Daniel Strong for taking me west after
the years I have spent looking east.

When I look back on it now, I recognize that
meeting the Mongolian consul opened the door to
Asia for me. I am thankful for the possibilities he
gave me, and thankful that he opened my eyes to a
whole new continent to discover. Mr. Brummelhuis
passed away in early September 2006. I would like
to dedicate this book to him.

MARCO VAN DUYVENDIJK

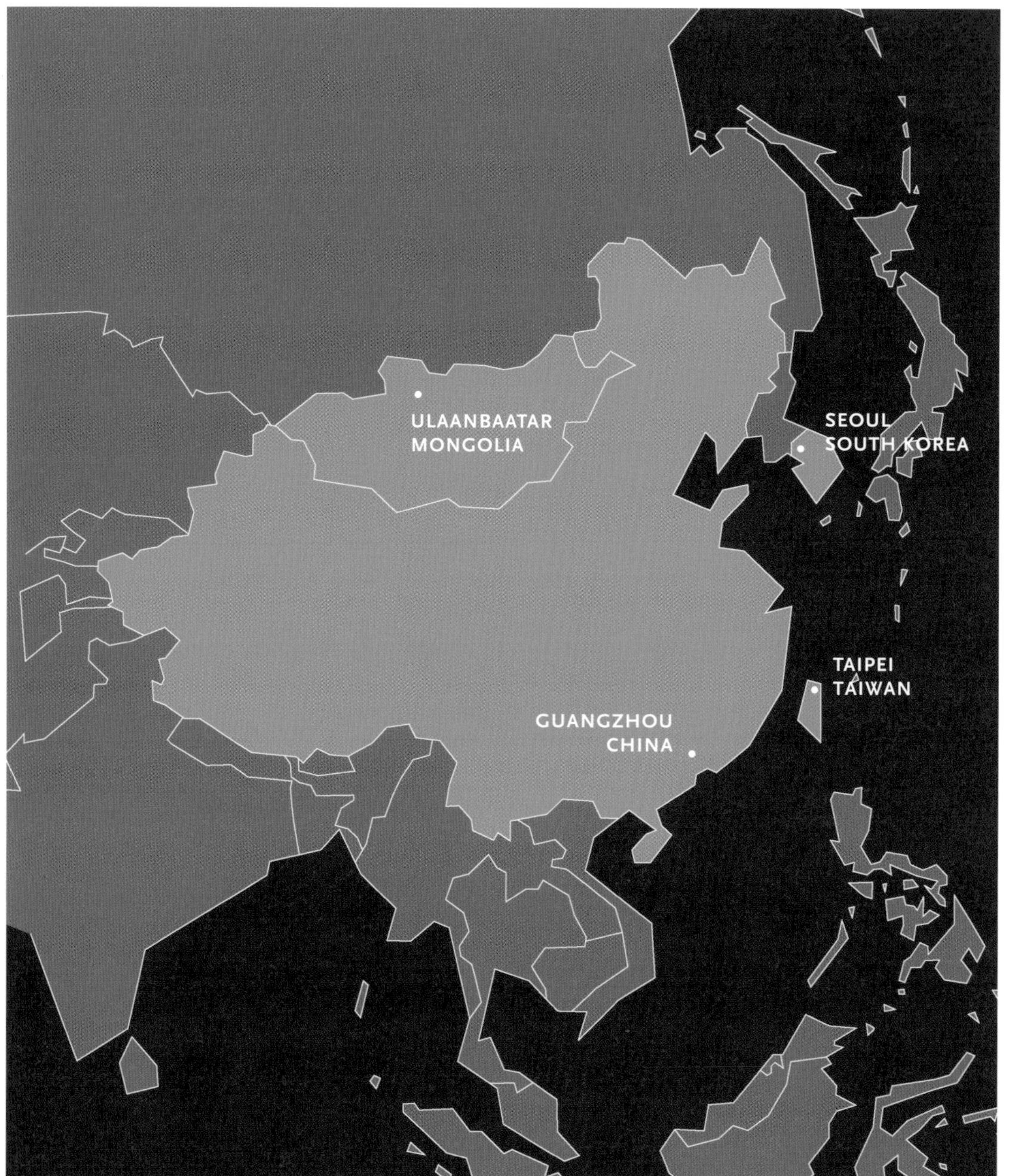

ULAANBAATAR
MONGOLIA
SEOUL
SOUTH KOREA
TAIPEI
TAIWAN
GUANGZHOU
CHINA

CONTENTS

CONTORTIONIST GIRLS
ULAANBAATAR, MONGOLIA 2004
13

ALTERNATIVE YOUTH
ULAANBAATAR, MONGOLIA 2004
27

**THE CITY OF GUANGZHOU AND
GUANGDONG PROVINCE**
CHINA 2005
43

BETEL NUT BEAUTIES
TAIWAN 2006
77

HIGH SCHOOLS
SEOUL, SOUTH KOREA 2006
103

LIST OF WORKS
126

CONTORTIONIST GIRLS

ULAANBAATAR, MONGOLIA 2004

Contortionists can bend their body in shapes that seem to defy the limits of what is physically possible. It has been said that they have physical abnormalities enabling them to do what they do, but reality is more down-to-earth. Natural disposition and skeletal build are factors that establish different limitations in each person, but age and regimen are more important.

Contortionism in Mongolia developed over centuries in the Buddhist monasteries, centers for education as well as theatre, music, and dance. During the Communist era, which began in Mongolia in 1924, contortionism became an important element in the Mongolian State Circus. Currently the State Circus is going through difficult times. After the collapse of Communism in 1990, state support of the Circus decreased in the context of an overall weak economy. The Circus building now looks neglected. Still, practice continues.

Odonchimeg, a contortionist twelve years of age, was four when she did her first exercises. During the day she attends a regular high school and in the afternoon she spends two hours at the Circus. At school her abilities surprise her classmates. "My friends say that it looks like I don't have bones."

Predictably, they ask if it hurts, but Odonchimeg seems more the stoic type. She says that in the beginning everything was difficult and sometimes painful, but now it is not so hard. "Everyone can learn this," she said.

Odonchimeg has not yet performed in the Circus. Erdenesuvd, now thirteen, made her debut on stage at age twelve. She was eight years old when she first saw contortionists on television and was so enthusiastic that her mother enrolled her in the Circus school. She now performs at the State Academic Theatre of Drama. When she thinks about the future she thinks about a career in the circus, preferably in a circus outside of Mongolia. The fame and spotlights of a foreign circus sound attractive in a country where the circus barely manages to survive.

If you see Erdenesuvd after rehearsal in her jeans and t-shirt it is difficult to imagine her testing the limits of human flexibility in her performance. She is modest and a bit shy. When asked what makes contortionism special she answers: "That I can bend my back; that is what I find most special."

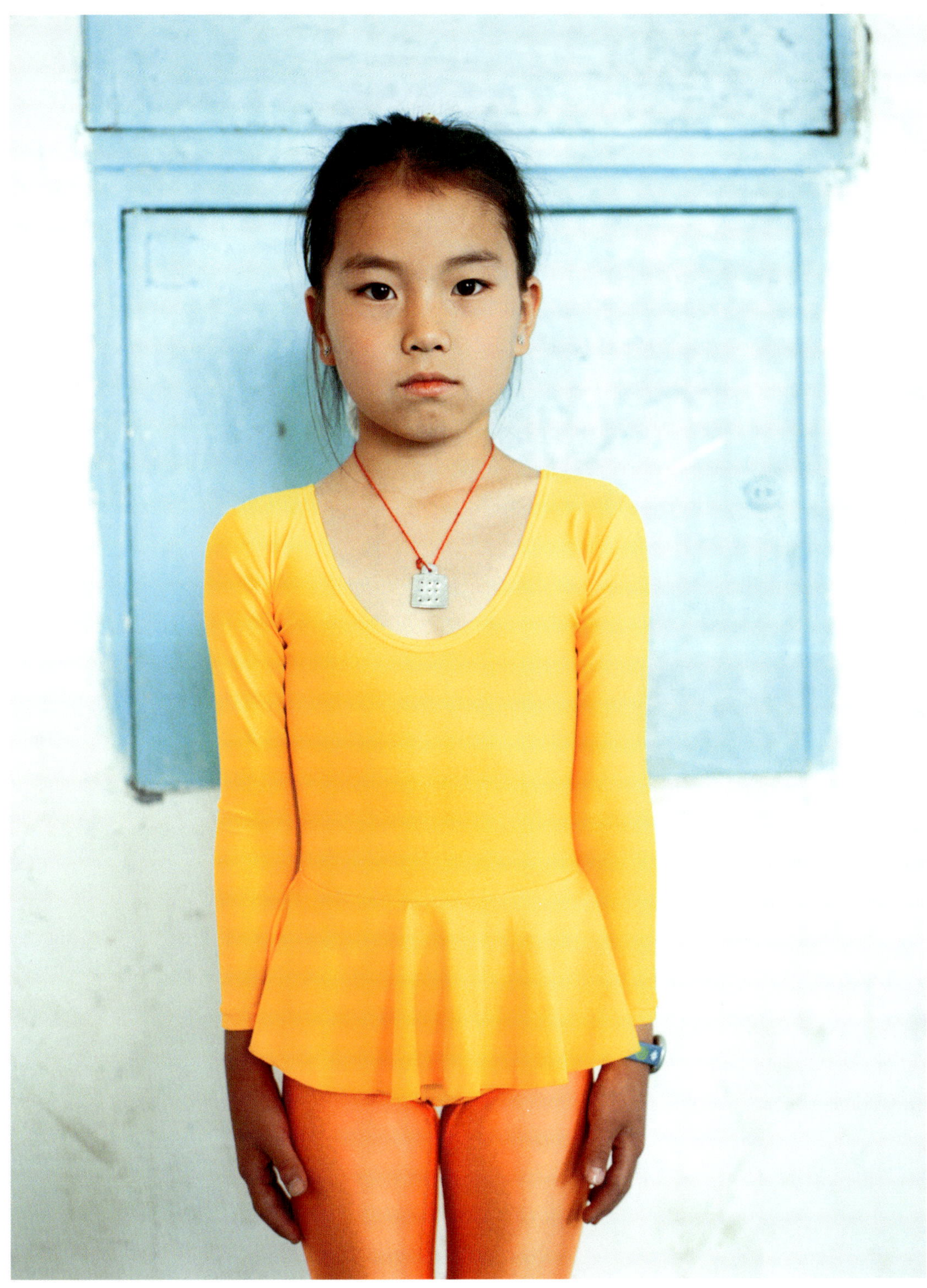

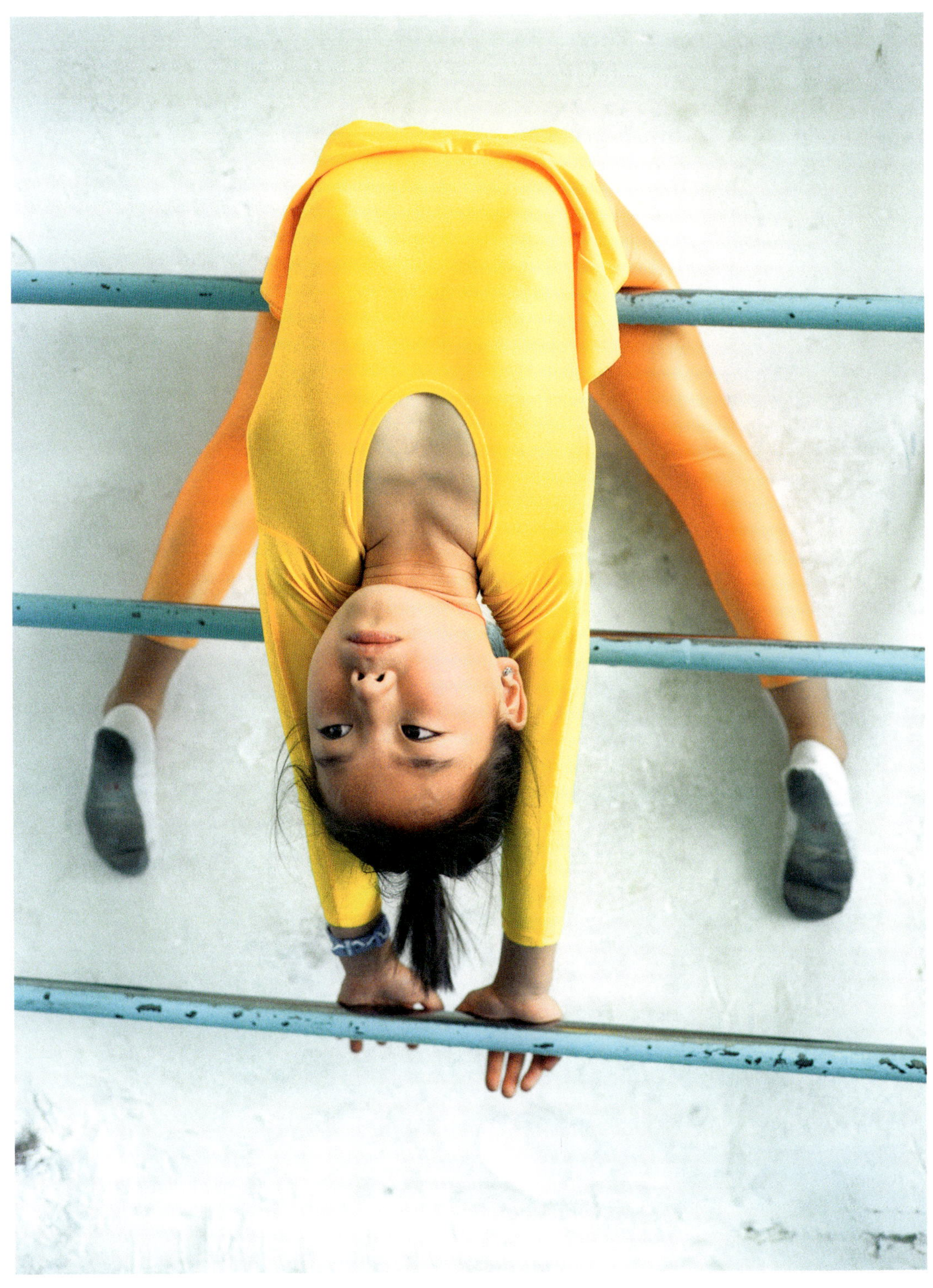

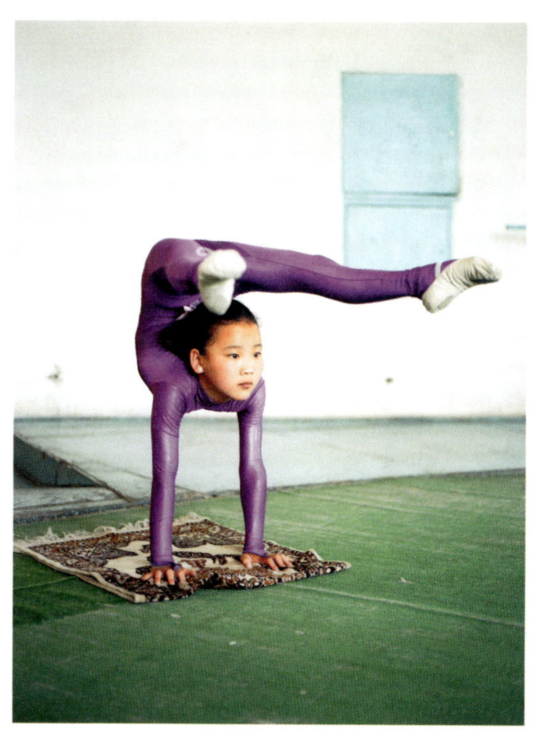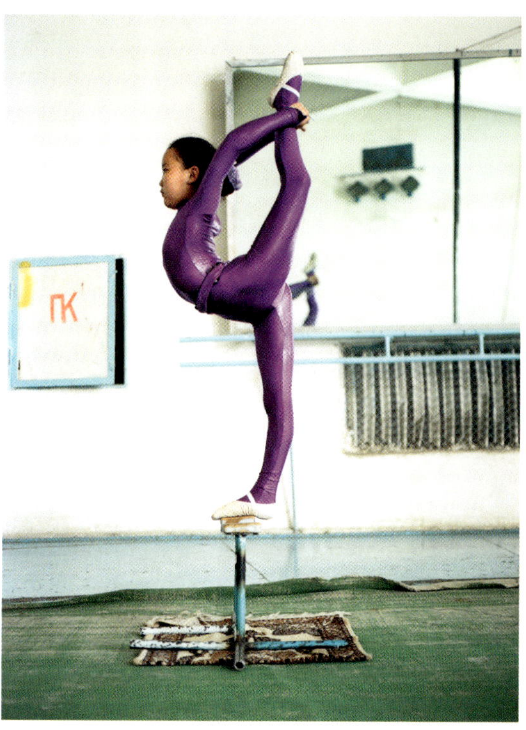
ПК

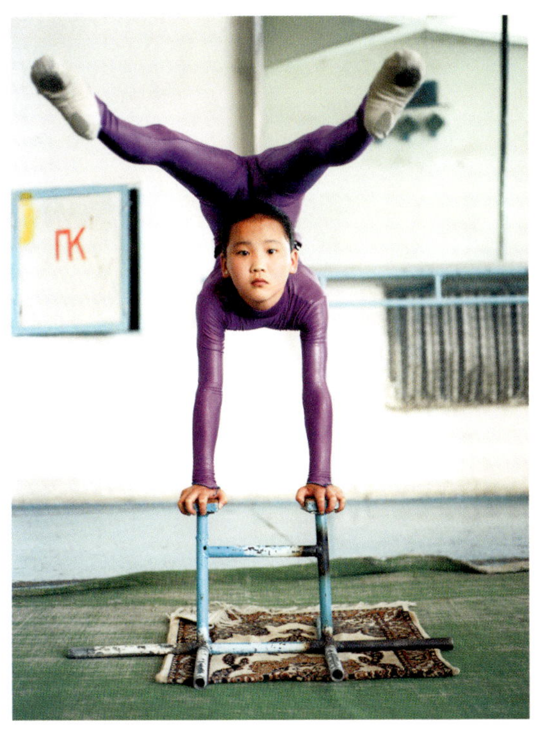

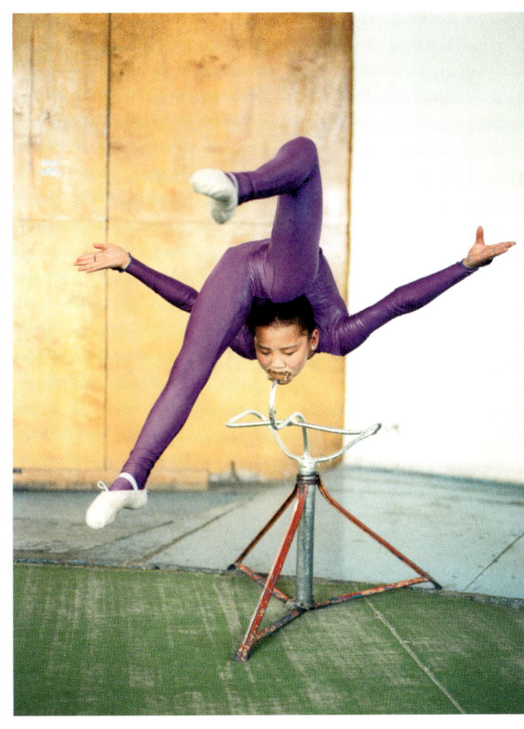

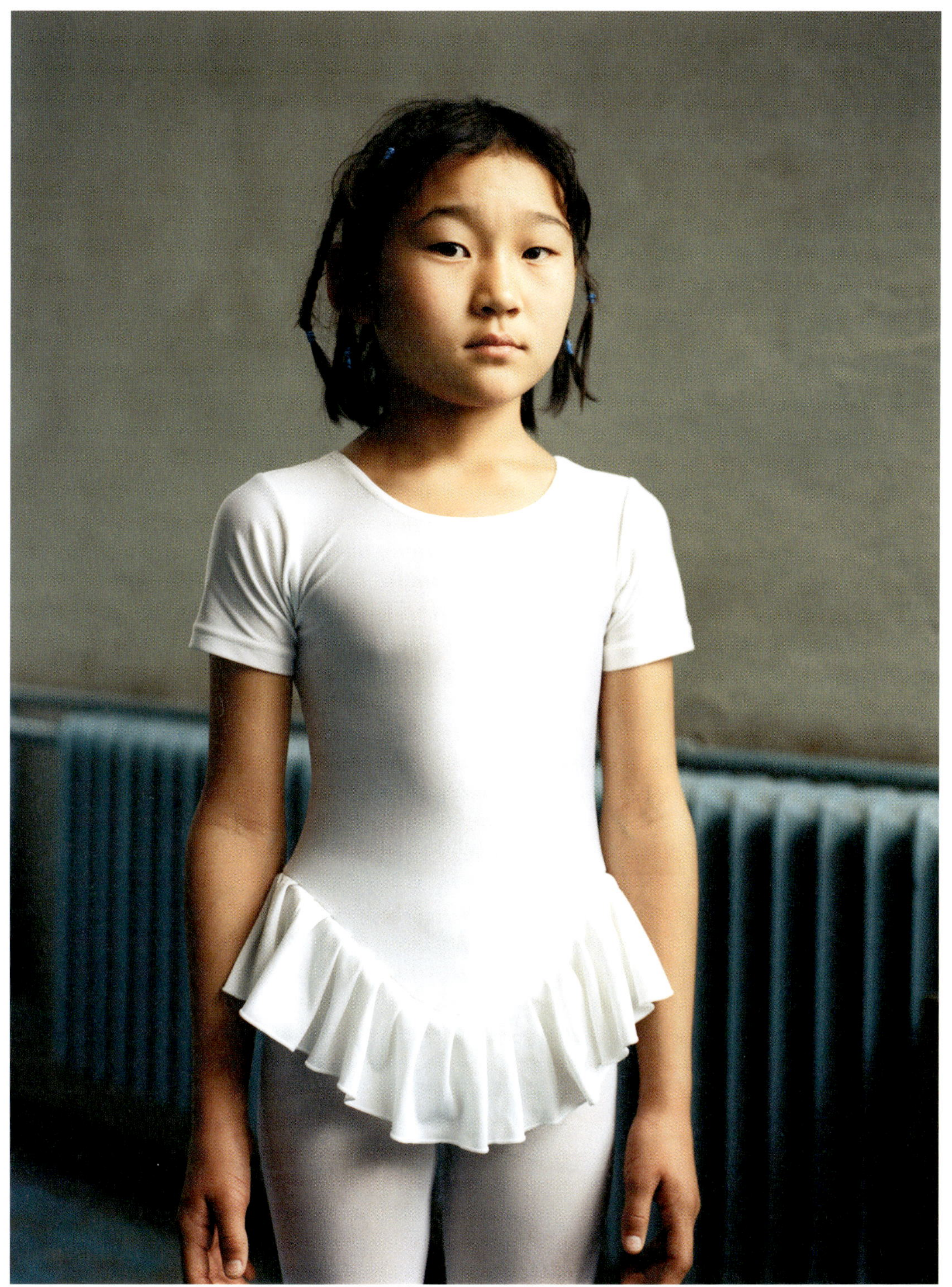

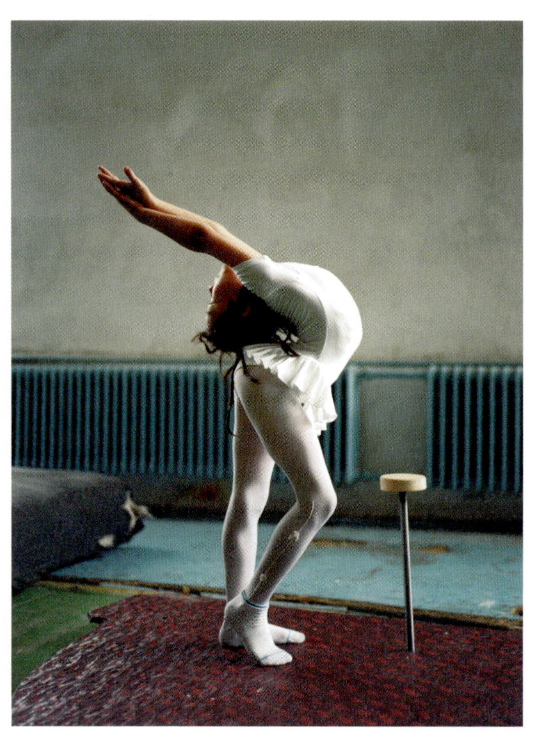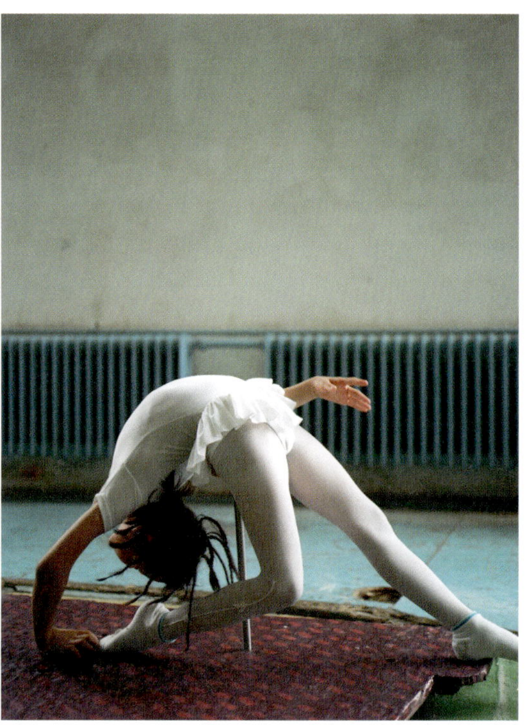

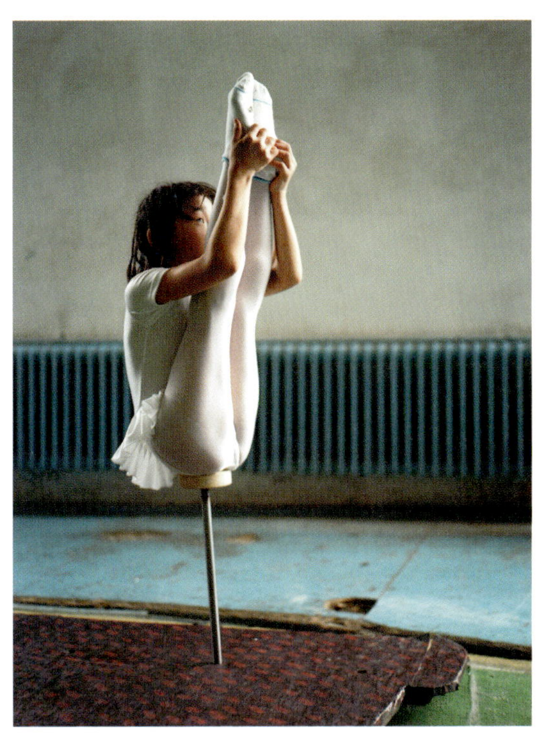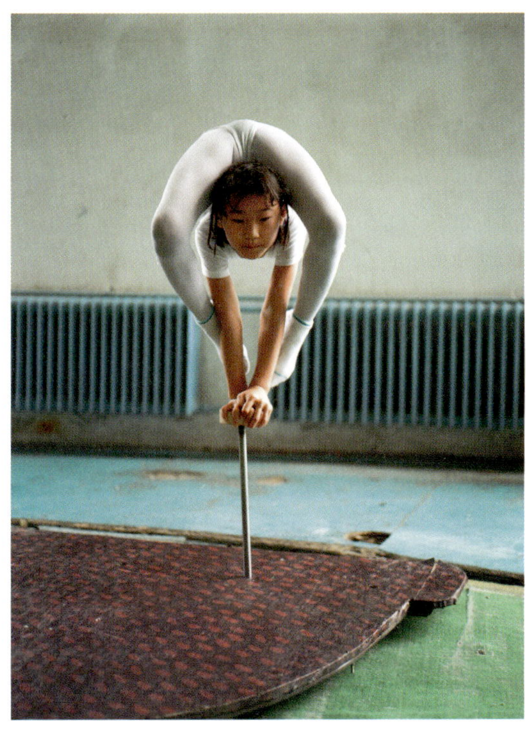

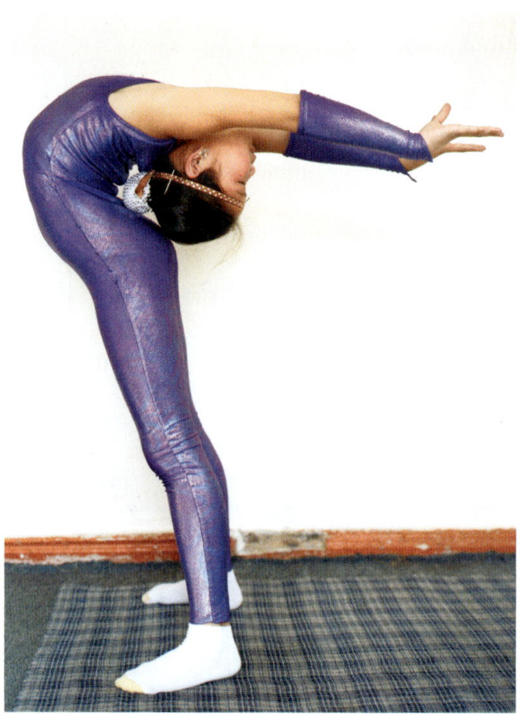 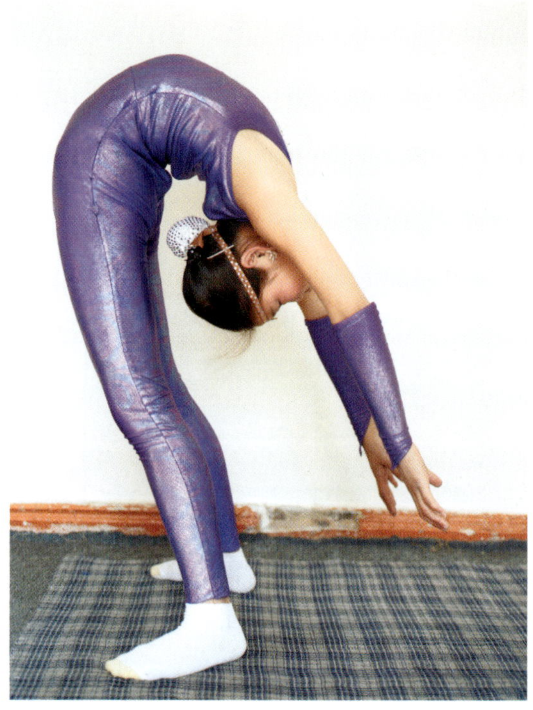

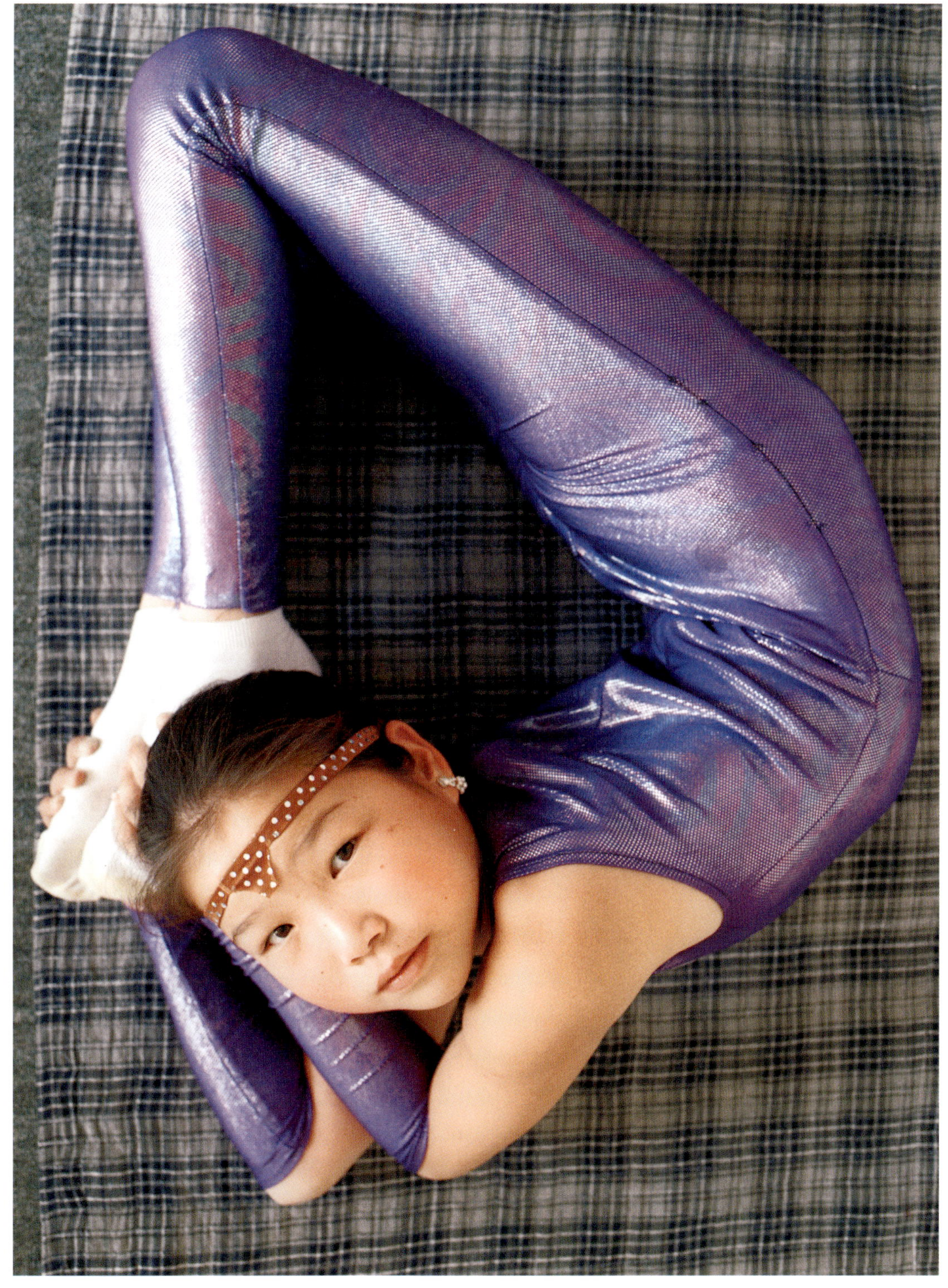

ALTERNATIVE YOUTH

ULAANBAATAR, MONGOLIA 2004

In size, Mongolia is nearly twice as big as the state of Iowa, but has a total population somewhat smaller (2.4 million Mongolians compared to 2.9 million Iowans). Half of the population is estimated to live in the capital city of Ulaanbaatar. While Ulaanbaatar was originally the spiritual center of Mongolia, with hundreds of Buddhist monasteries and temples, this changed when Mongolia became the world's second Communist republic. In the past seventy years Ulaanbaatar has become a city dominated by concrete blocks of flats. In these flats, following the silent revolution of 1990, the first generation of Mongolia's alternative youth has grown up.

Ulaanbaatar is by far the biggest city in Mongolia, but in a global sense it is still rather isolated. Popular bands do not include Ulaanbaatar in their world tour. However, with the presence of cable television, the Internet, and shops full of pirated copies of the latest CDs and DVDs, it has become as easy for young people in Ulaanbaatar to learn about trends and fashions as it is for people in Amsterdam or New York. But there are big differences as well. Urban culture is relatively new to Mongolians. If you ask young people in Ulaanbaatar about family history, most are only one or two generations away from a nomadic existence. The situation of physical isolation combined with "virtual" immersion in world youth culture makes the youth of Ulaanbaatar a self-made generation. If they like fashion styles from Japan, Europe or the USA, they likely make their own versions. If they want to go to concerts, it means they first have to start their own bands. Tattoo and piercing shops are a recent development and this generation is the first in Mongolia to experiment with these forms of self-expression.

Having grown up surrounded by the concrete of Ulaanbaatar, they consider themselves city-dwellers and admit that they would have a hard time going back to nomadic life. But all of them have family in the steppes and speak with respect and dignity about nomadic traditions. Ochgerel, a boy with long black hair and white extensions, is one example. Two years ago he lived three months as a shepherd. "It was beautiful to live how people lived in this country for centuries unchanged, but I must admit that it was a bit boring sometimes. Even if I met the most beautiful nomadic woman of Mongolia in the steppes, I would not stay there. I would take her to the city." Ochgerel now spends his time playing guitar in a metal band.

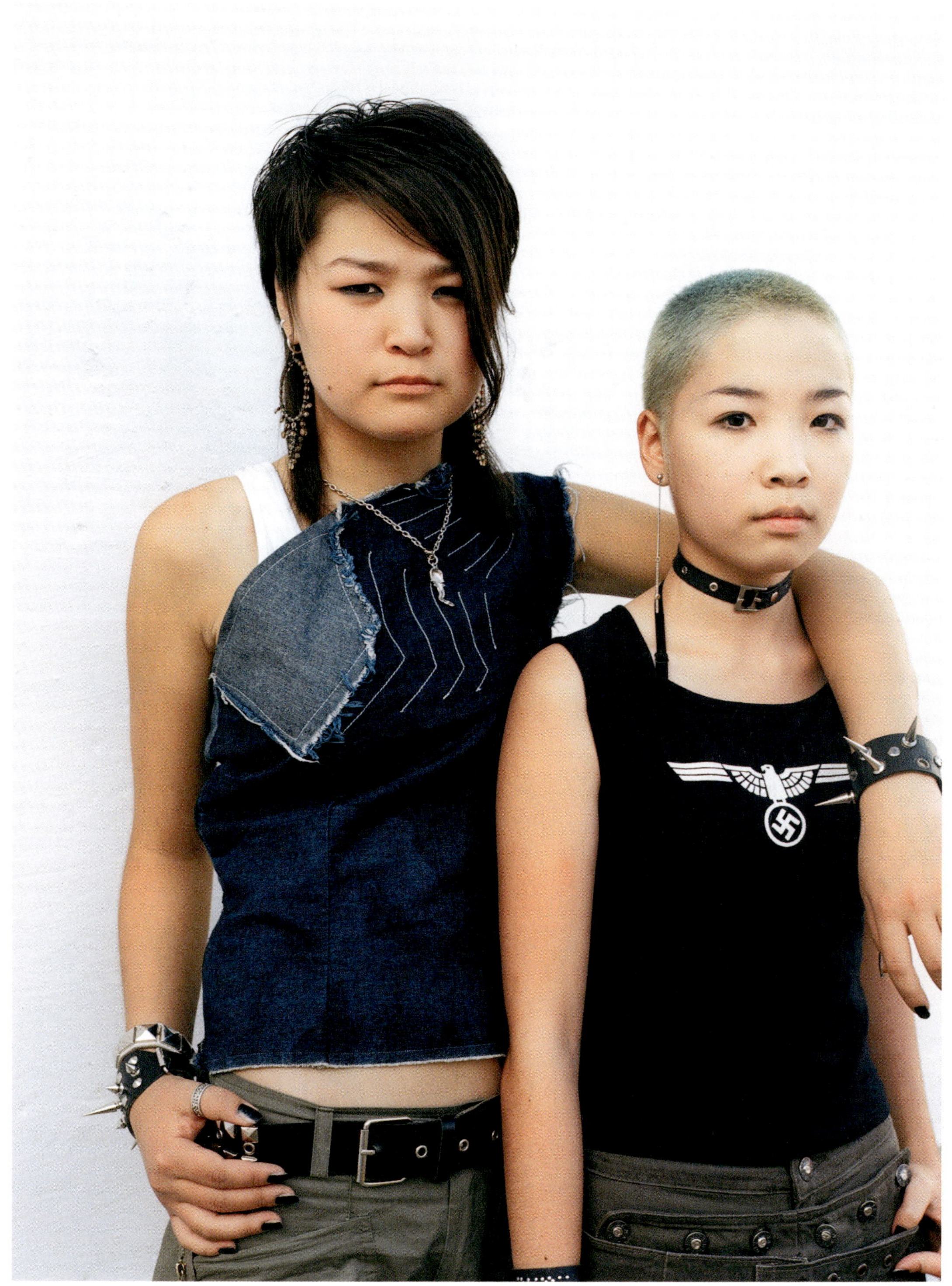

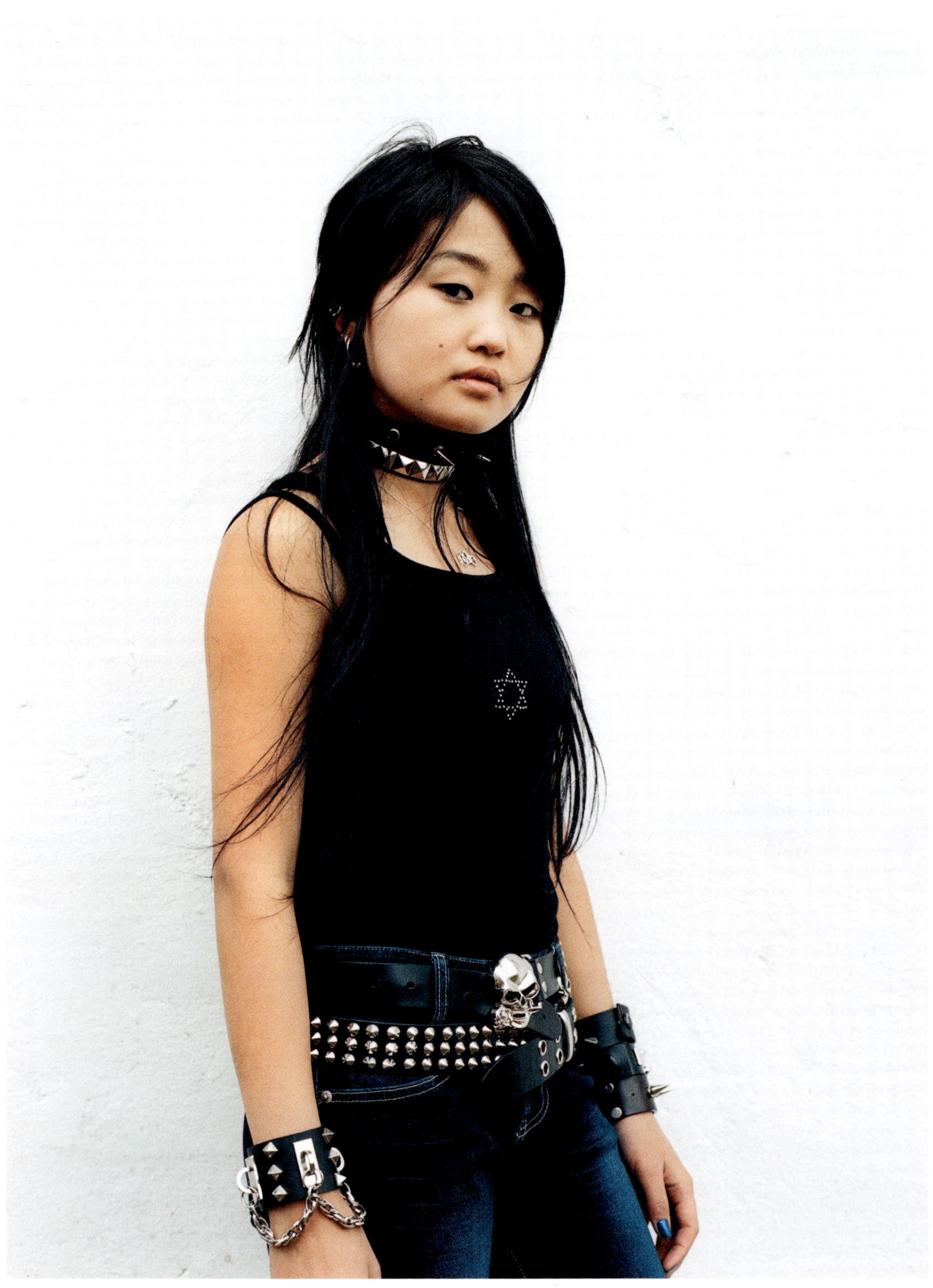

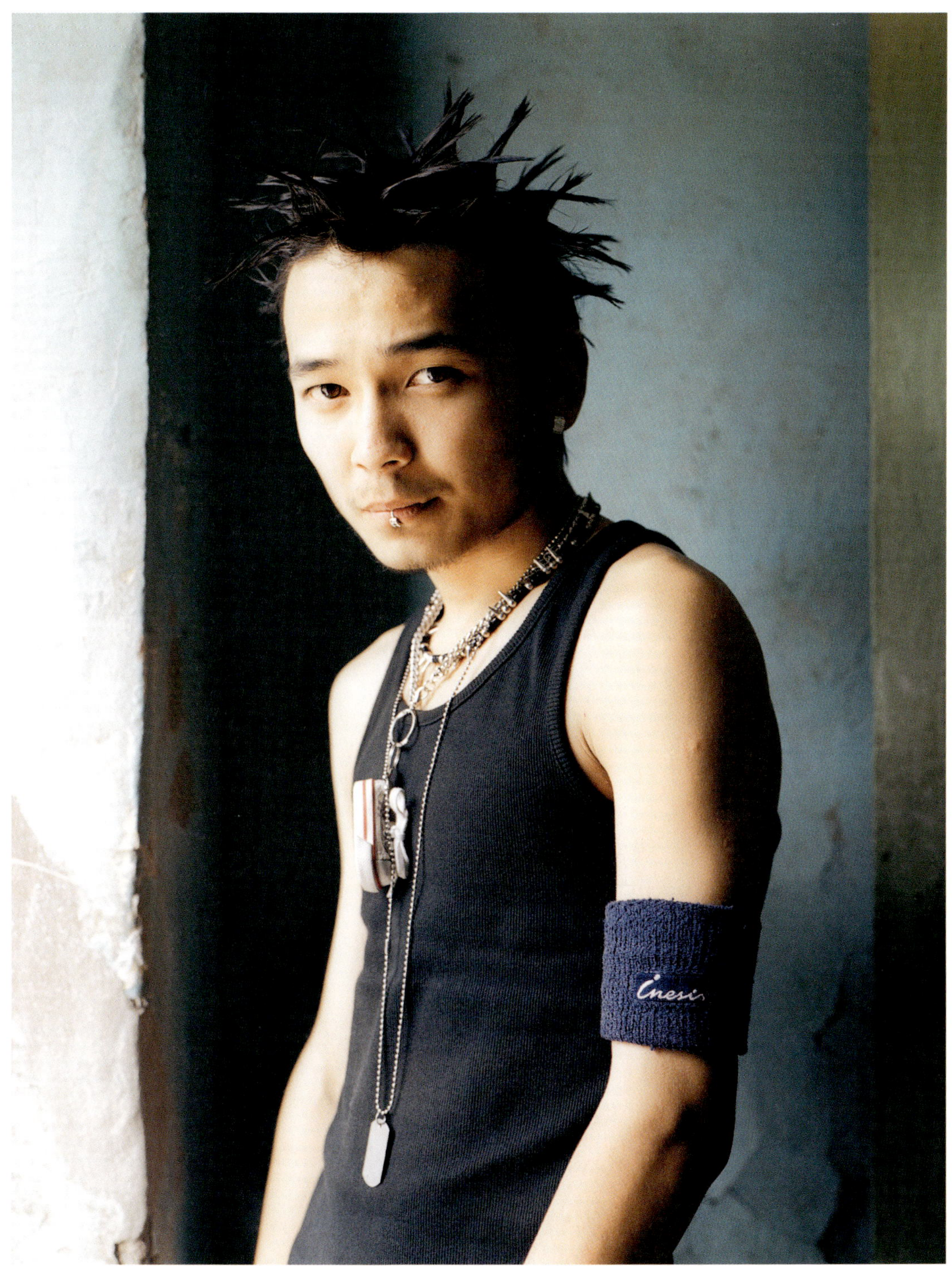

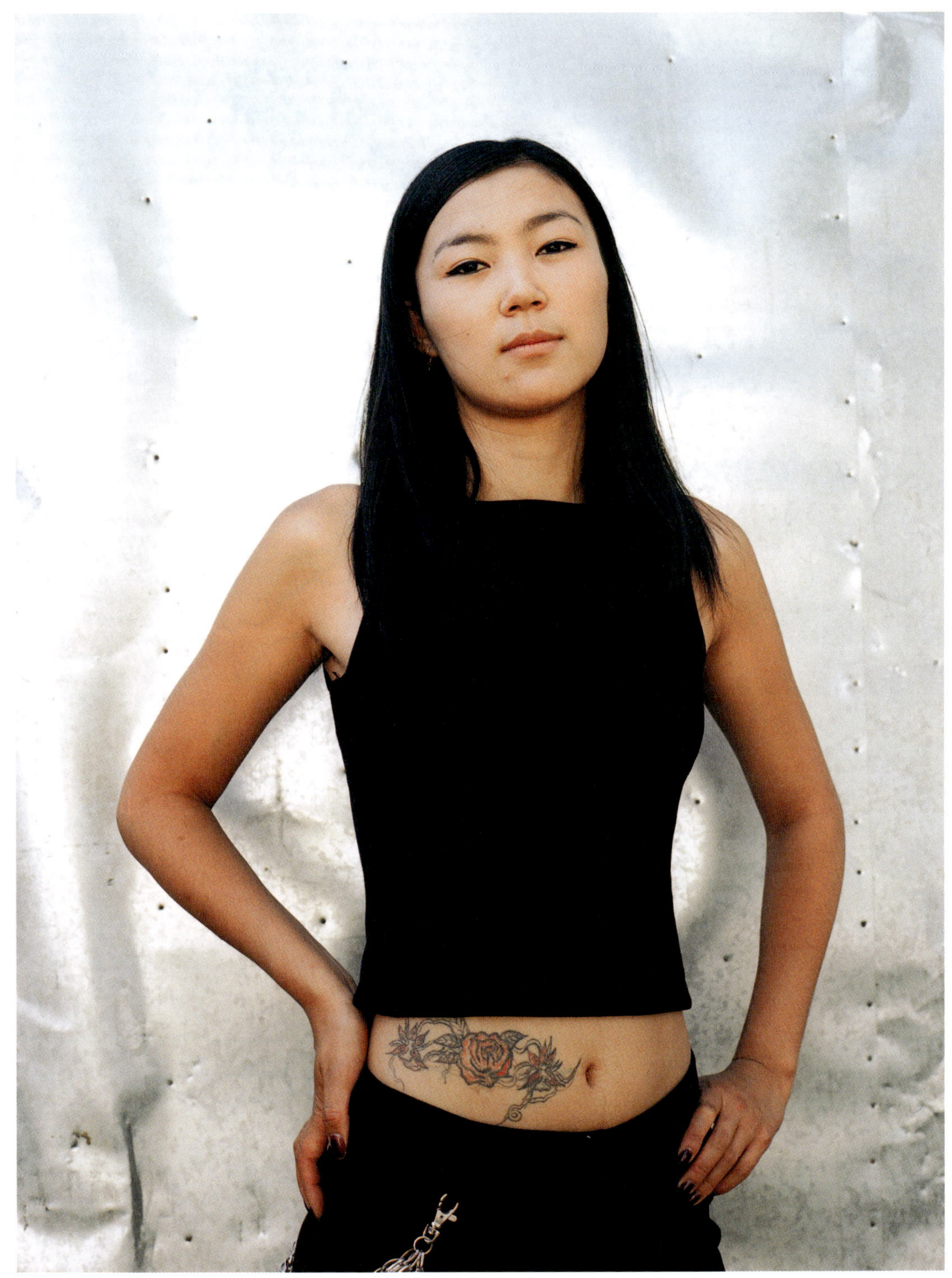

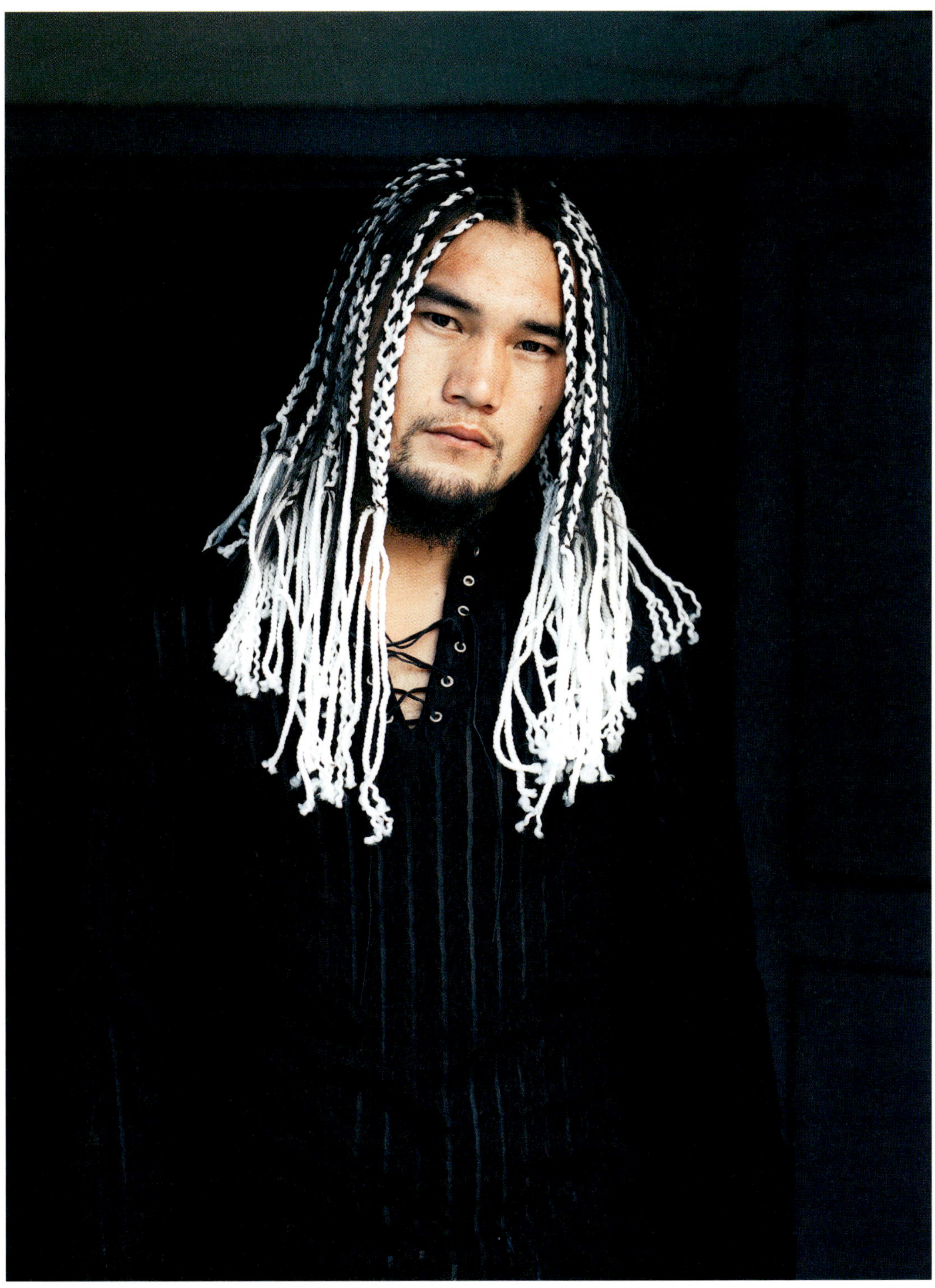

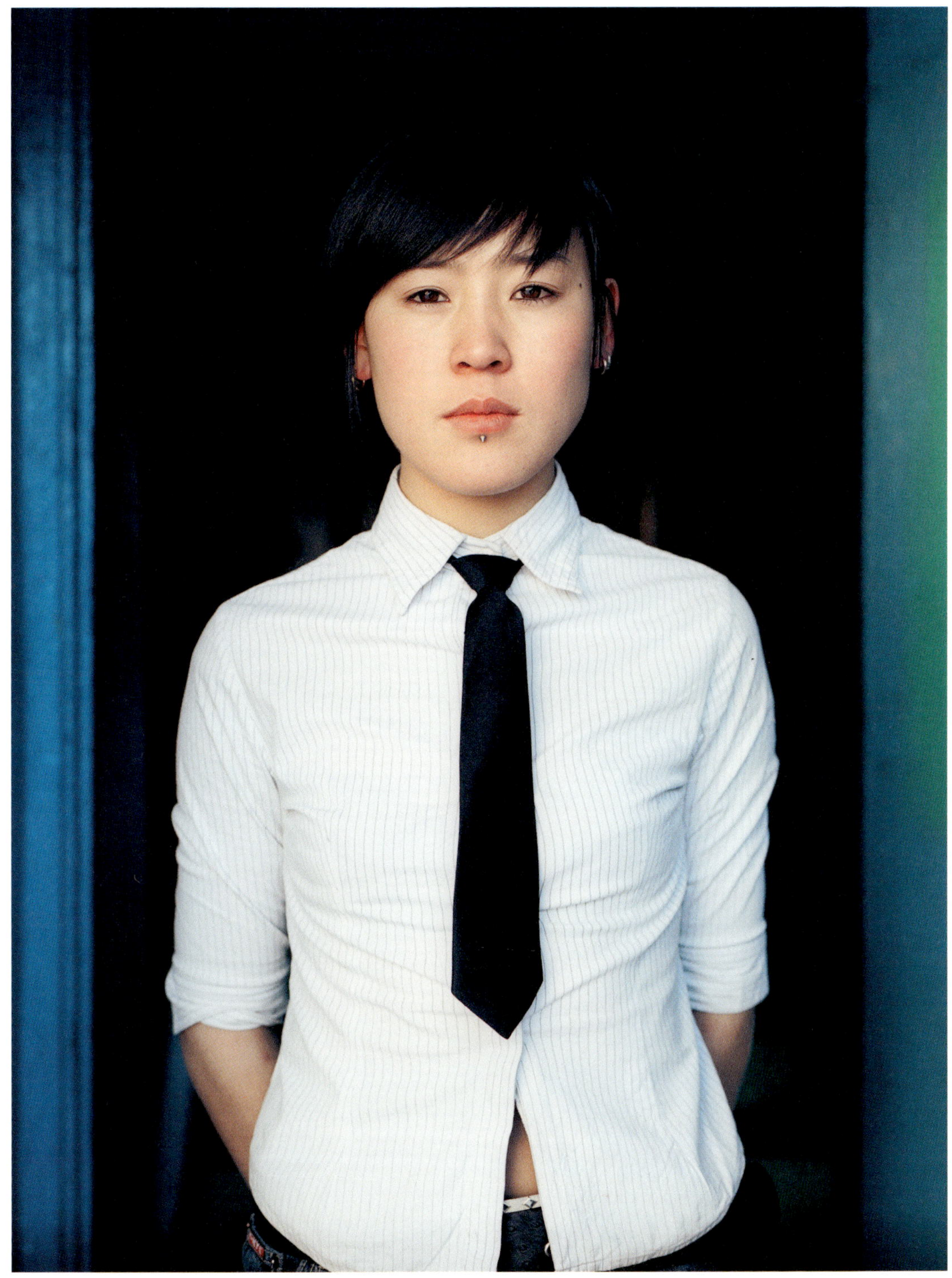

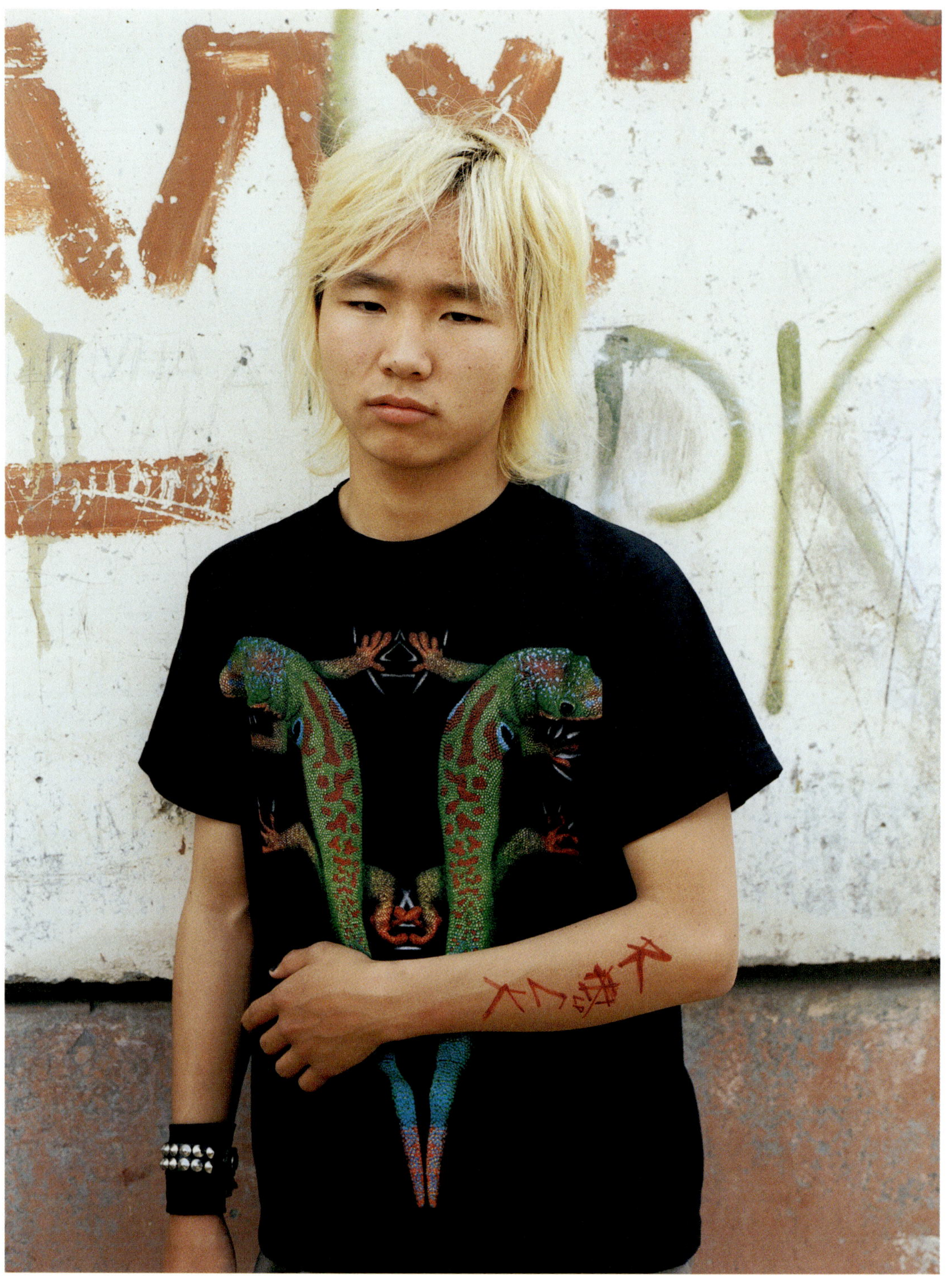

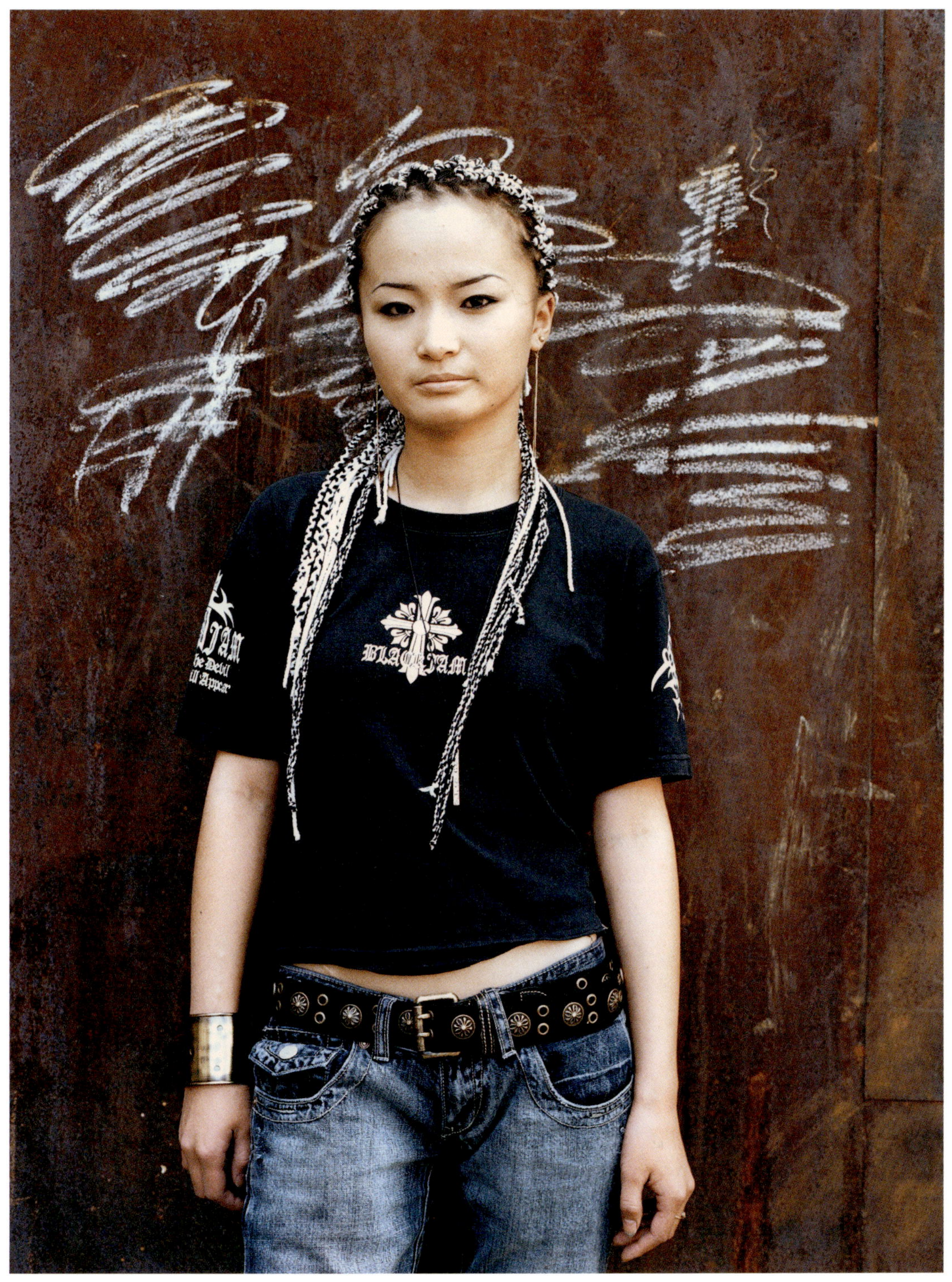

BLACK JAM
the Devil
Will Appear
BLACK JAM

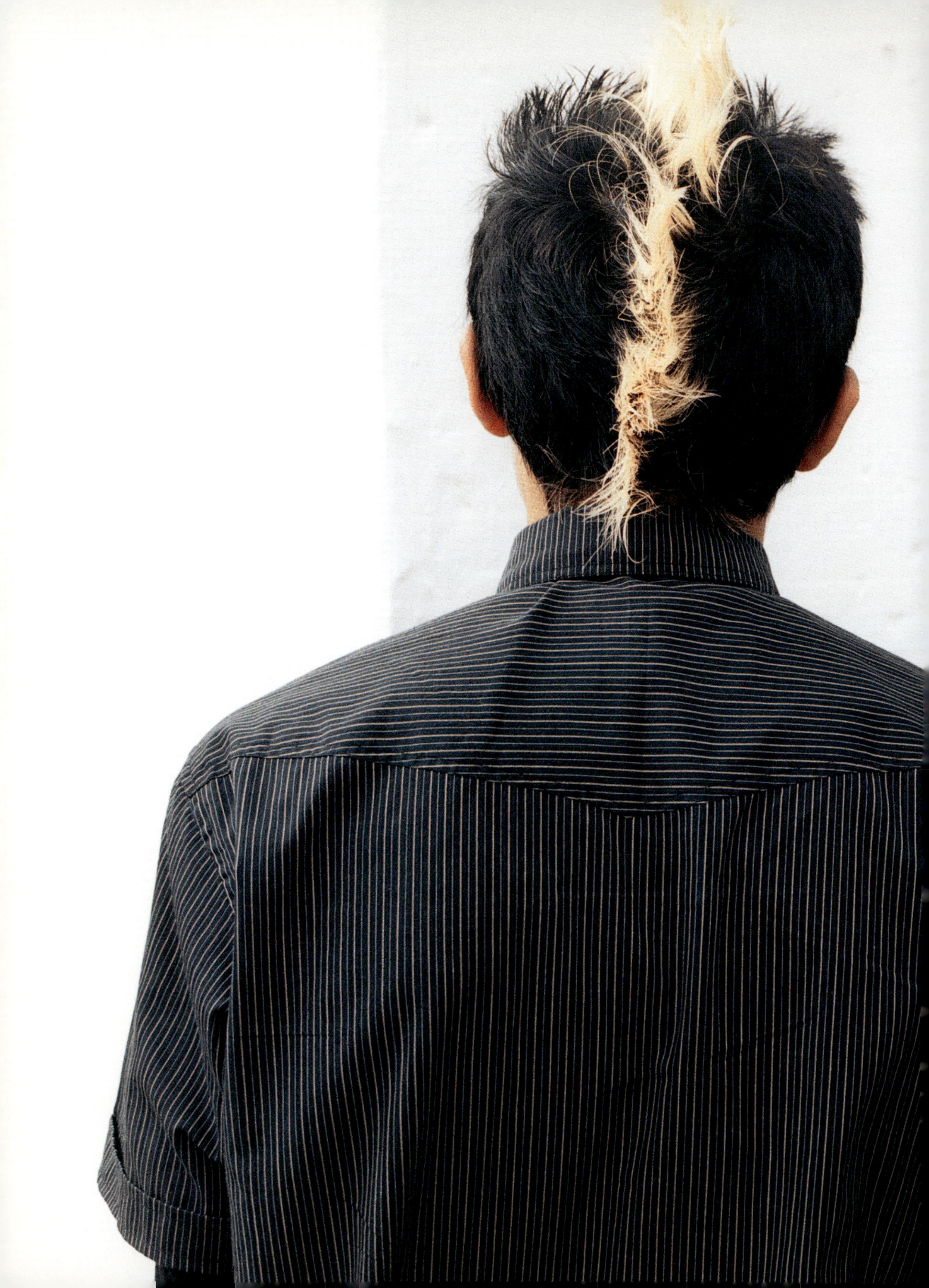

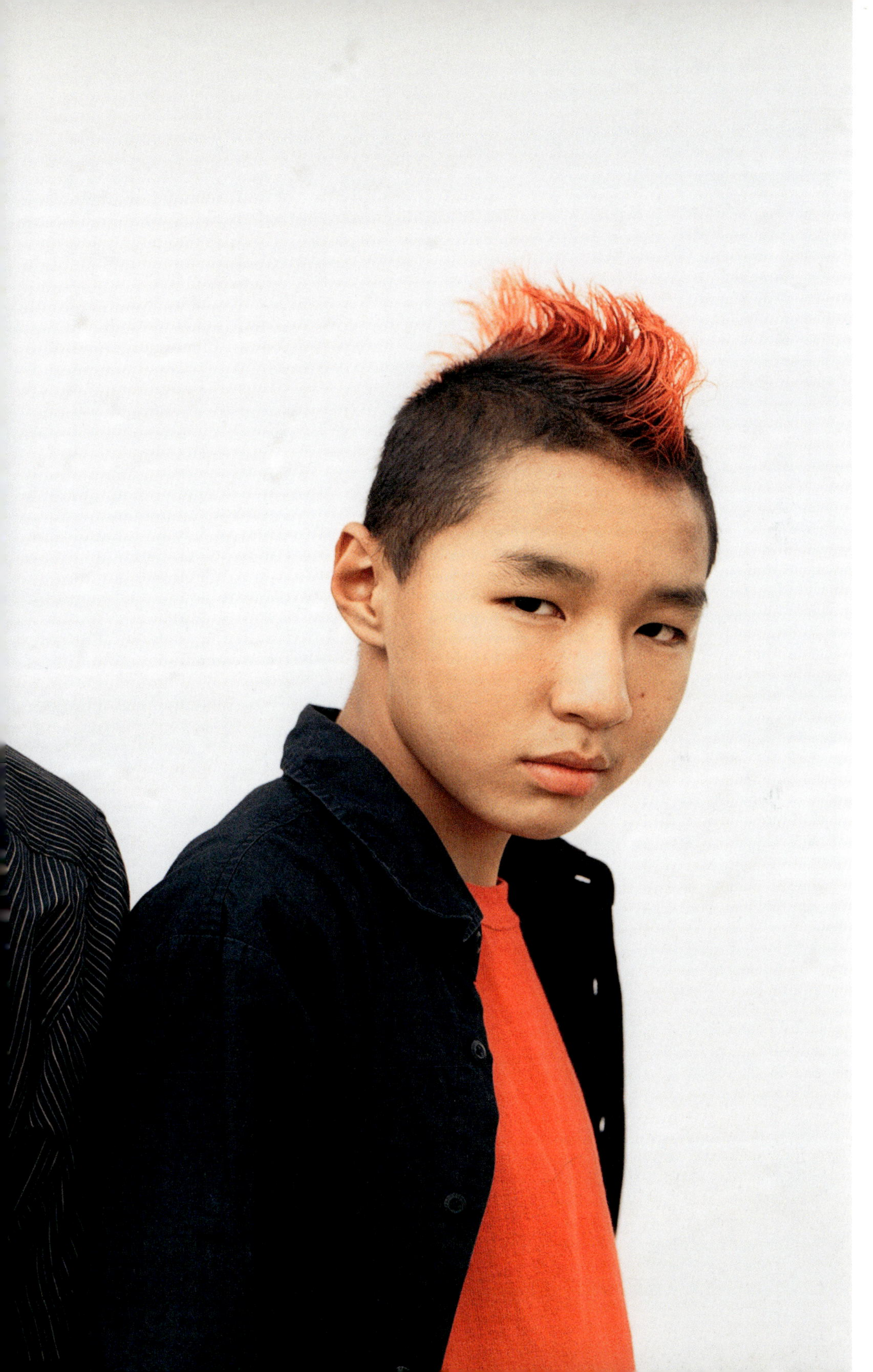

THE CITY OF GUANGZHOU
AND GUANGDONG PROVINCE

CHINA 2005

The past three years I lived with my girlfriend as caretakers at Oud-Amelisweerd, an estate on the outskirts of Utrecht. This country house, under supervision of the Centraal Museum in Utrecht, was built in 1770, and remains to this day, to a large extent, in its original condition. Entering Oud-Amelisweerd is like stepping back in time. The house breathes history; its unpolished, run-down beauty breathes mystery.

In the 18th century, trade between the Chinese city of Canton and the Netherlands was extensive. In those days it became fashionable in Europe for wealthy families to have Asian items such as silks, china, and wallpaper in their homes. In keeping with fashion, two rooms in Oud-Amelisweerd were decorated with 18th century hand-painted Chinese wallpapers. While most such wallpapers in private houses have disappeared over the years, in Oud-Amelisweerd they remain. It is now the only place in Europe where two rooms of hand-painted Chinese wallpapers can be found in their original location and in good condition.

In spring 2005 I developed the idea to make a photographic series loosely inspired by the wallpapers. I traveled to Canton, currently known as Guangzhou, where the wallpapers were originally painted. Having been inspired by an old country house in the Netherlands—where romantic ideas from the 18th century about country life and nature, as well as a fascination for exotic cultures, still abound—I found in 21st-century Guangzhou a tension between urbanization and nature. Guangzhou is now a concrete jungle with seven million inhabitants and resembles only vaguely the scenes depicted on the 18th century wallpapers. As a result, I found my approach during this project less documentarian than usual. I was working more by association than with a clearly defined subject. In retrospect, other influences beyond wallpaper seem to have worked their way into the photographs.

For the first time in my life I was living in a city inhabited by seven million people, which made me think about the work of Hungarian photographers like Eva Besnyö, who moved to Berlin in the 1920s (and later to the Netherlands), and André Kertész, who first moved to Paris in 1925 and emigrated to New York in 1936. The work of both photographers reflects their impressions of these modern cities. Their photographs possess a dimension of weightlessness, an emphasis on structure and

different perspectives, which I tried to adapt in my
work. The films of Hong Kong-based director
Wong Kar-Wei—"In the Mood for Love", for
example—also had an impact on my photographs
in Guangzhou.

With this diversity of influences I may have
invented my own China as the project developed.
Everything fell into place when I returned
home and exhibited the works in the rooms of
Oud-Amelisweerd.

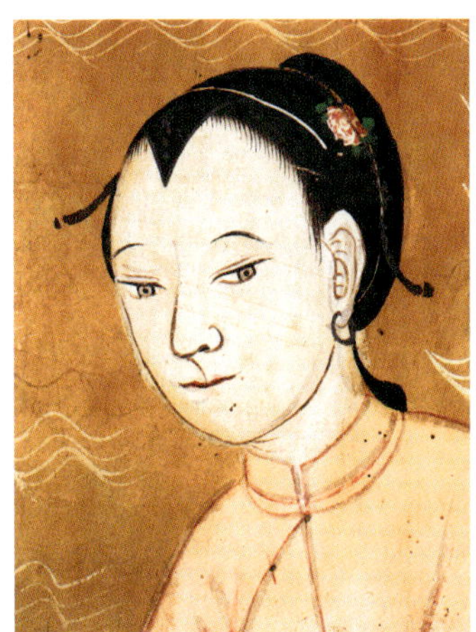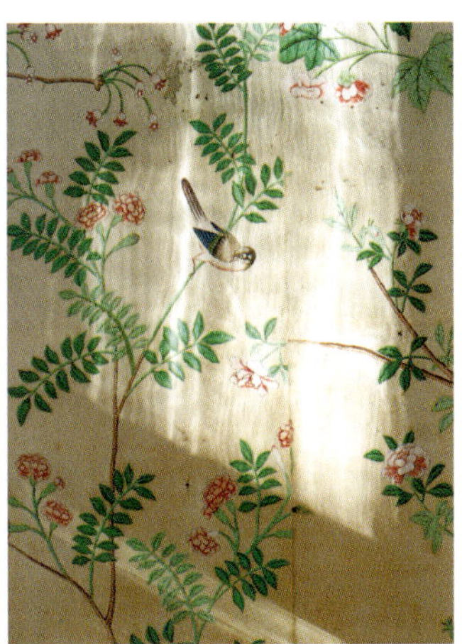

Details of Chinese wallpaper
Oud-Amelisweerd, The Netherlands

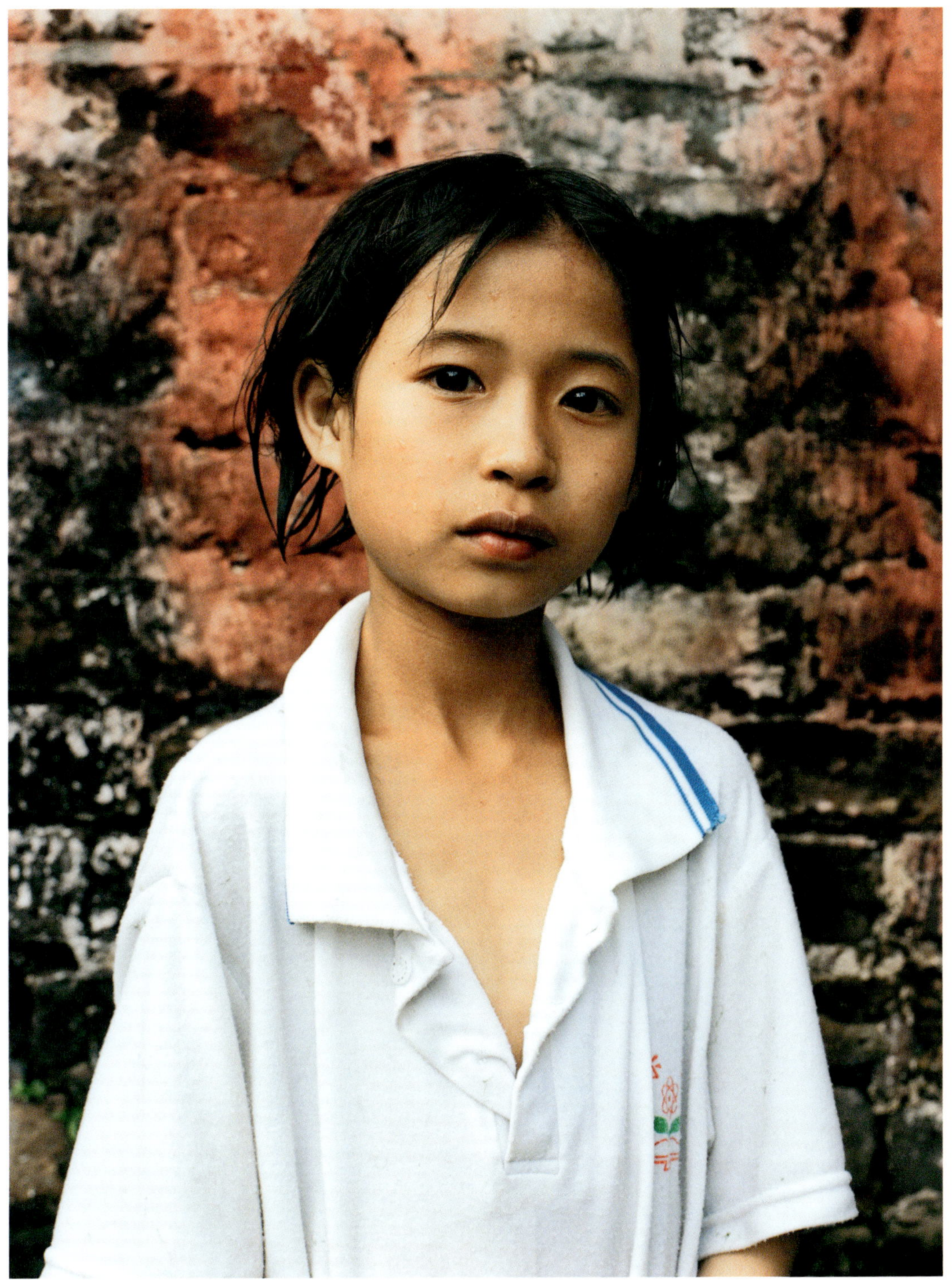

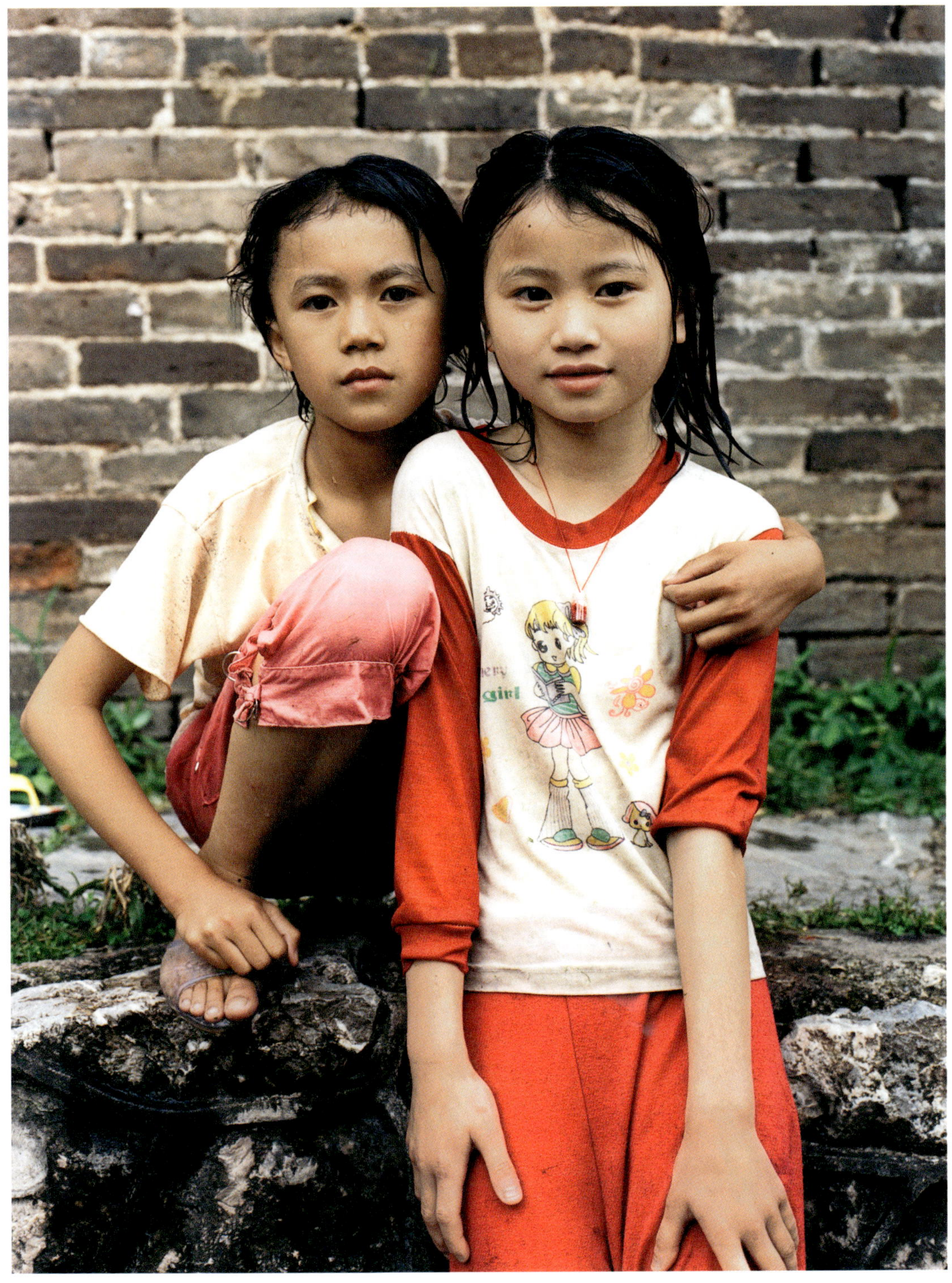

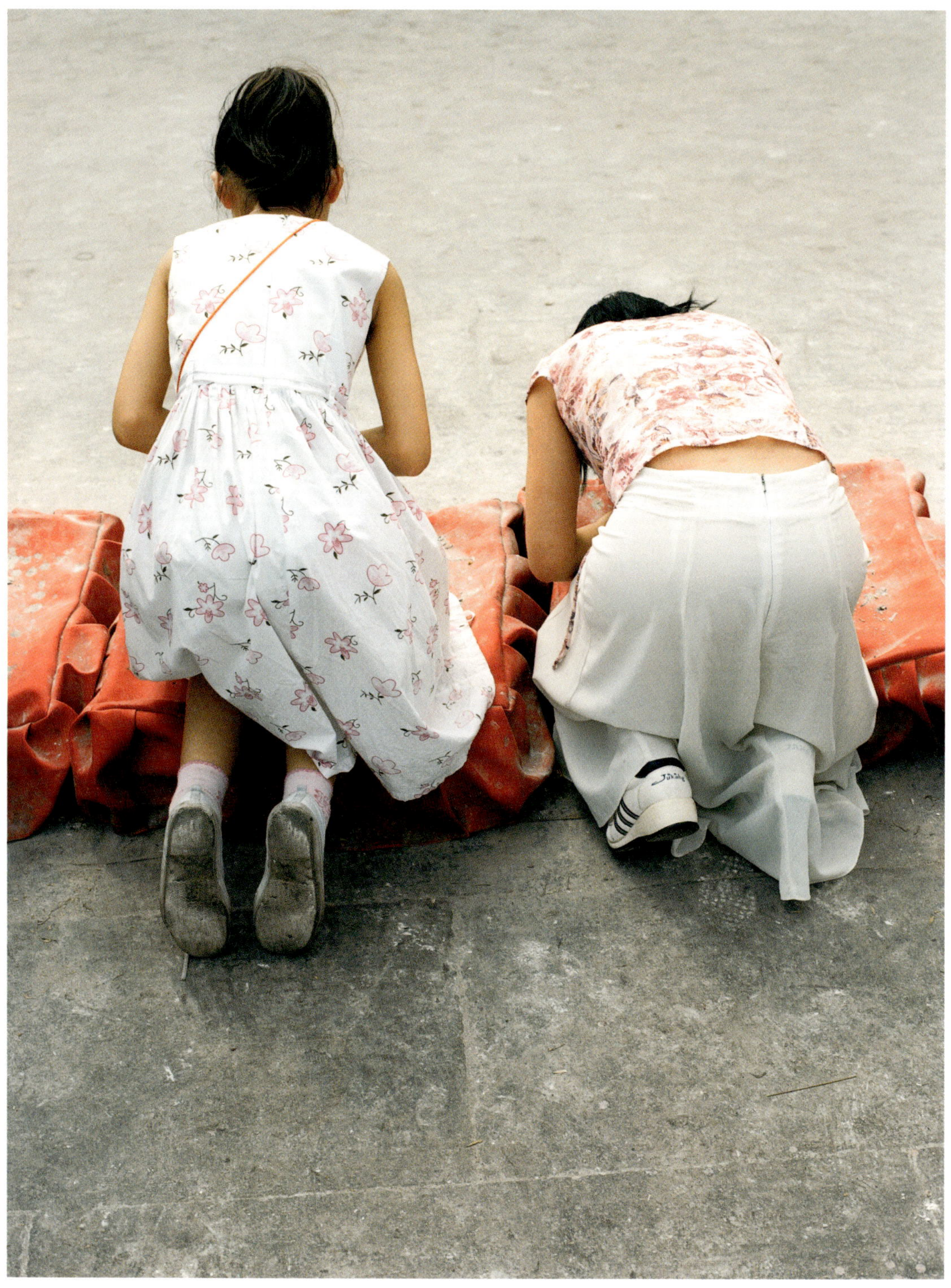

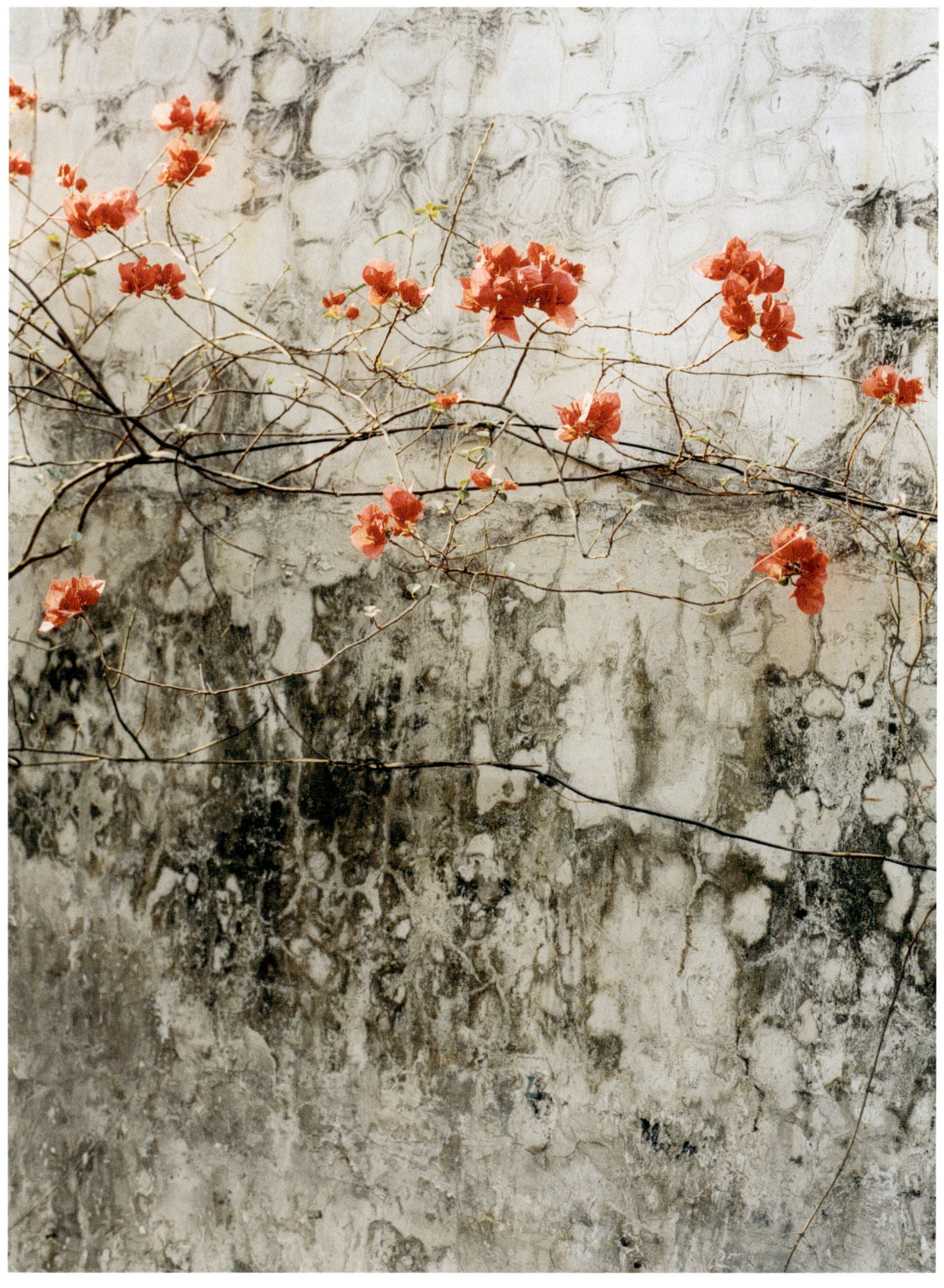

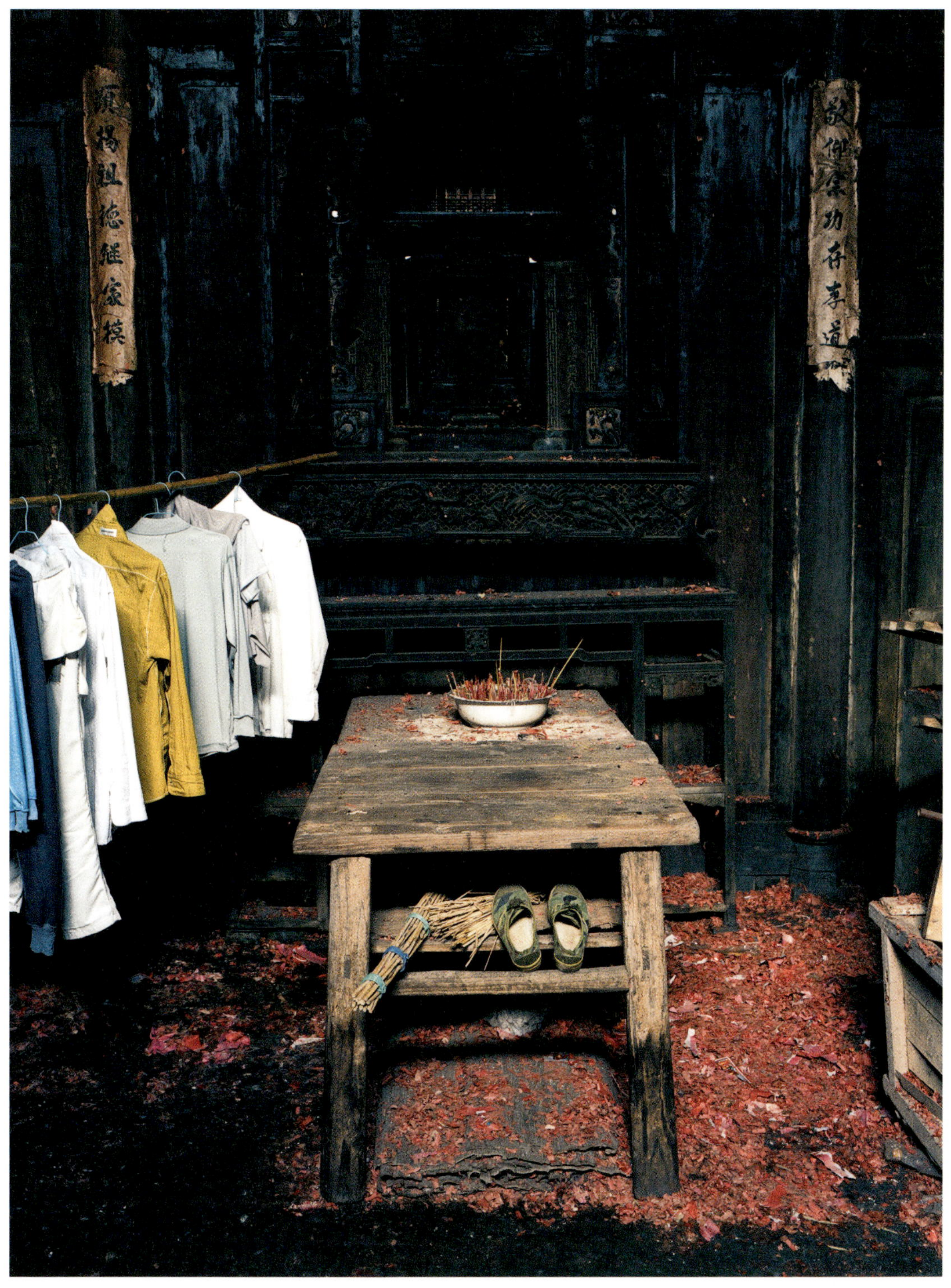
願揚祖德繼家模
敬傳宗功存孝道

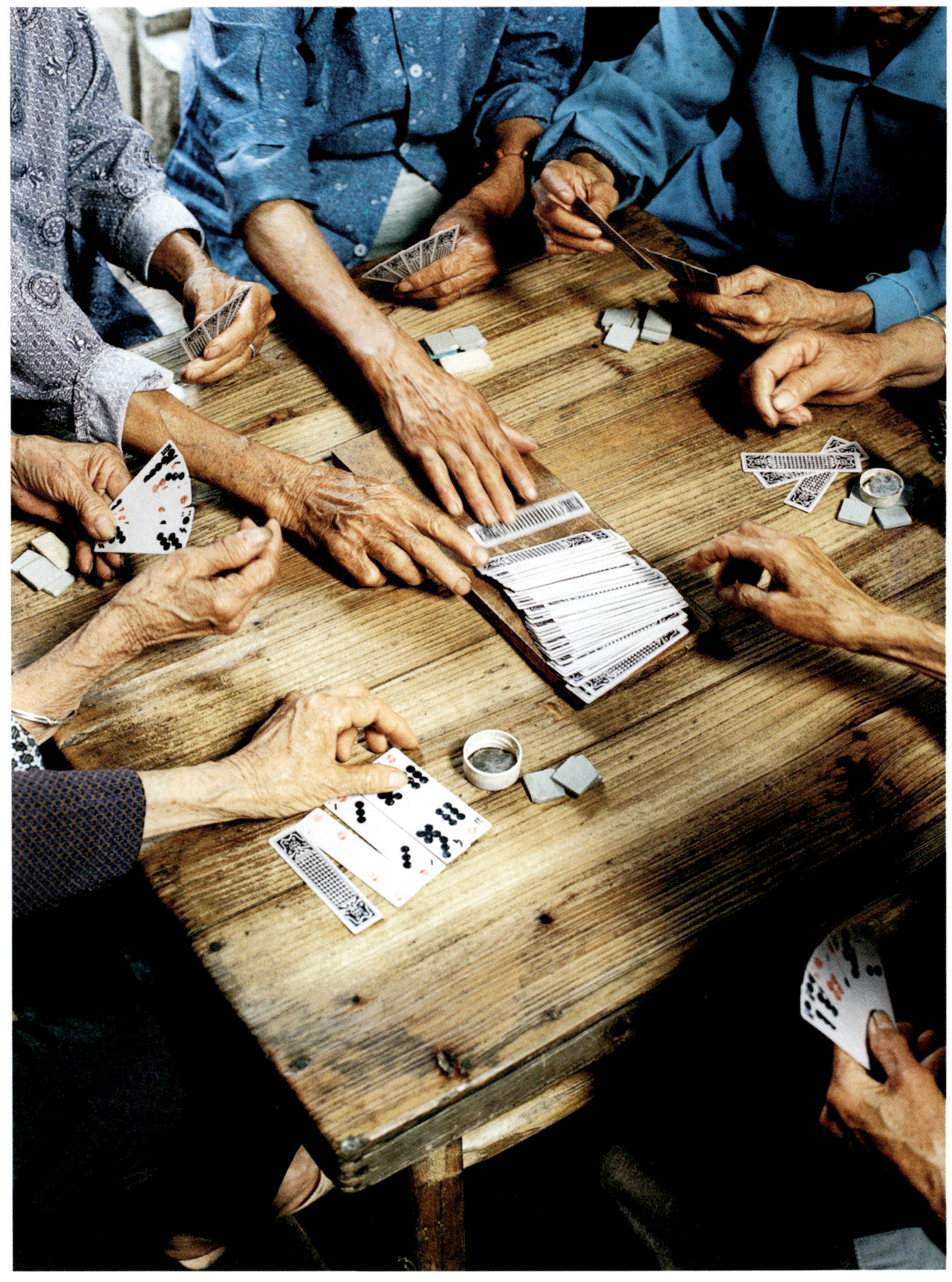

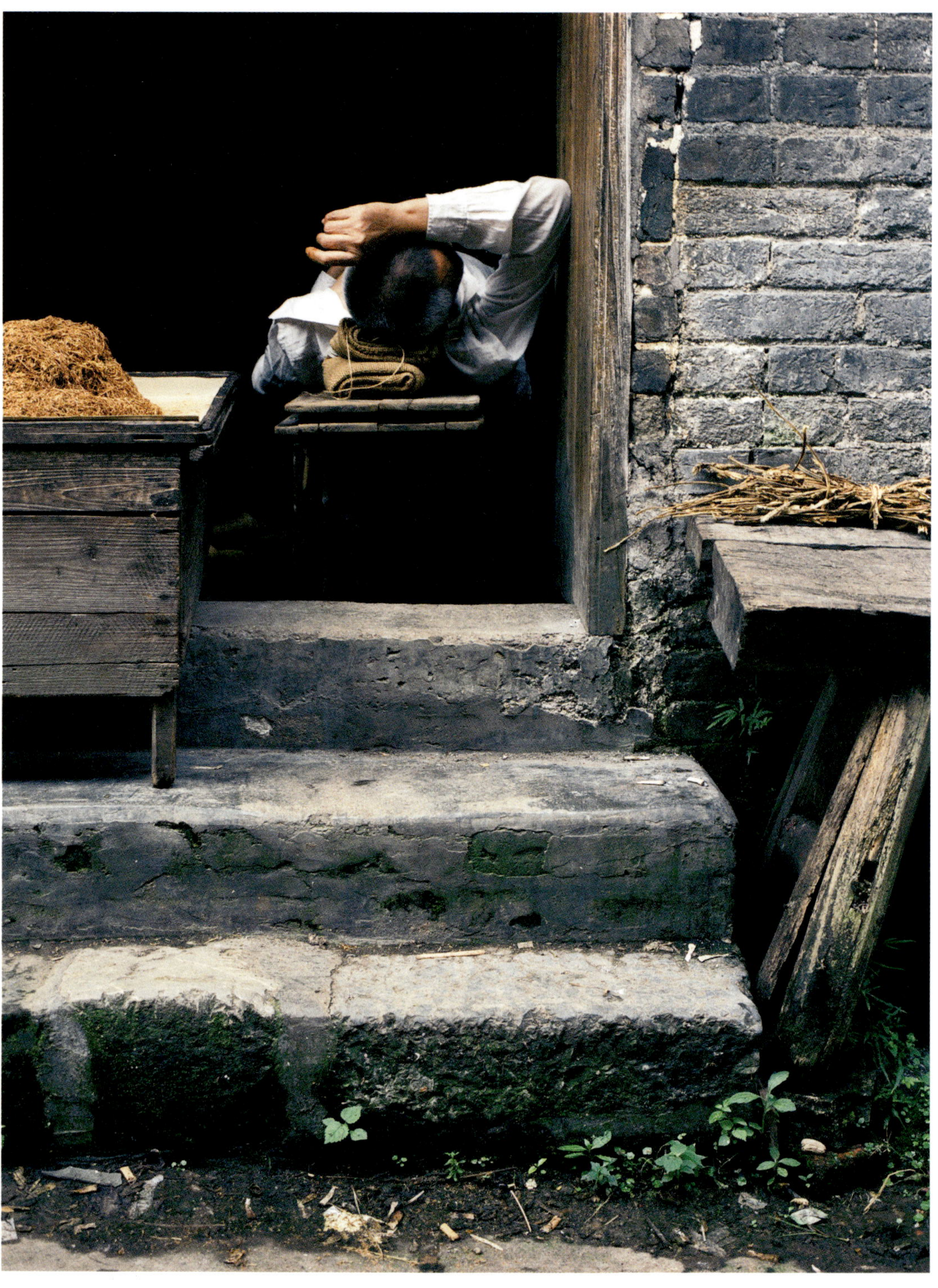

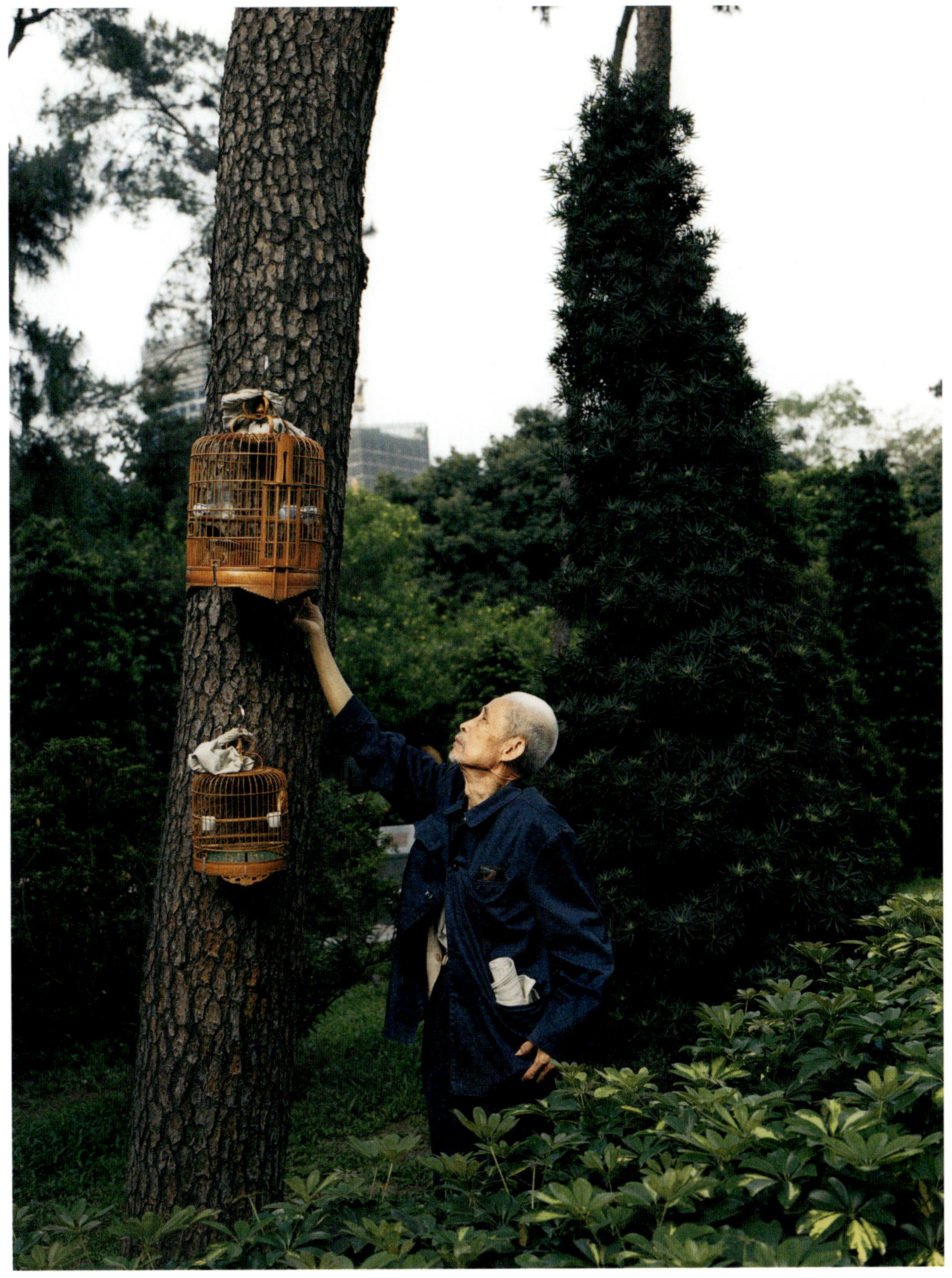

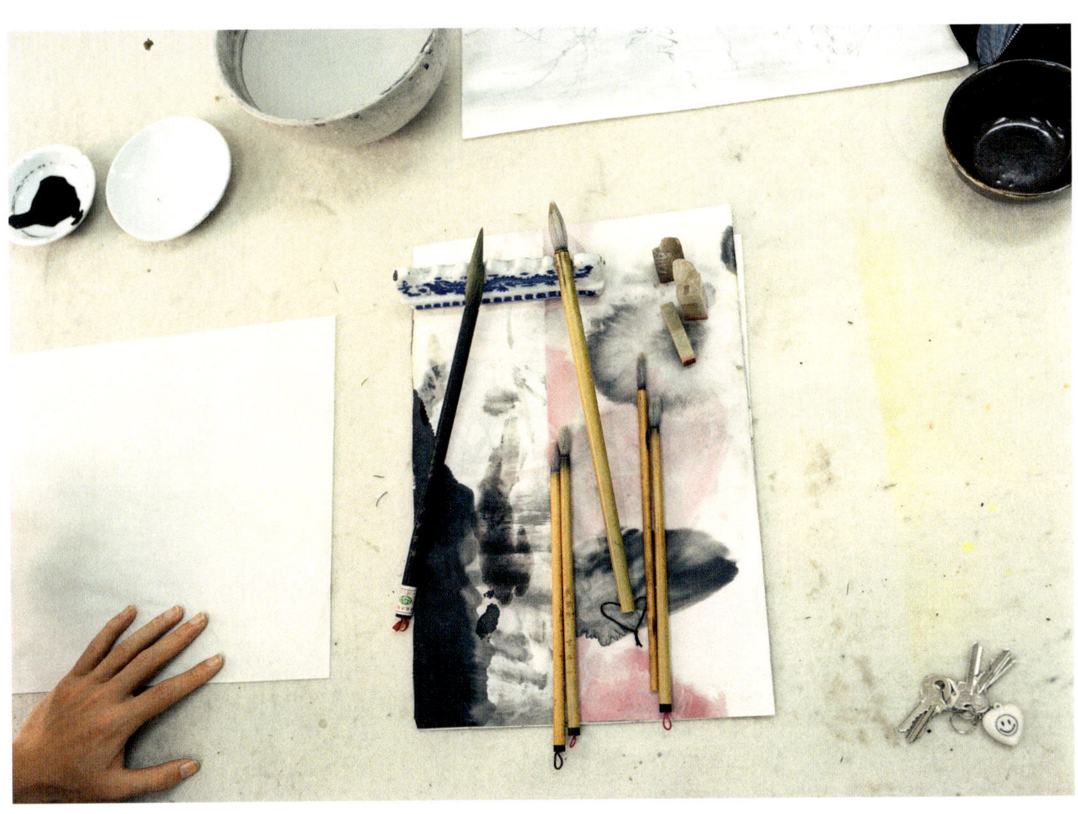

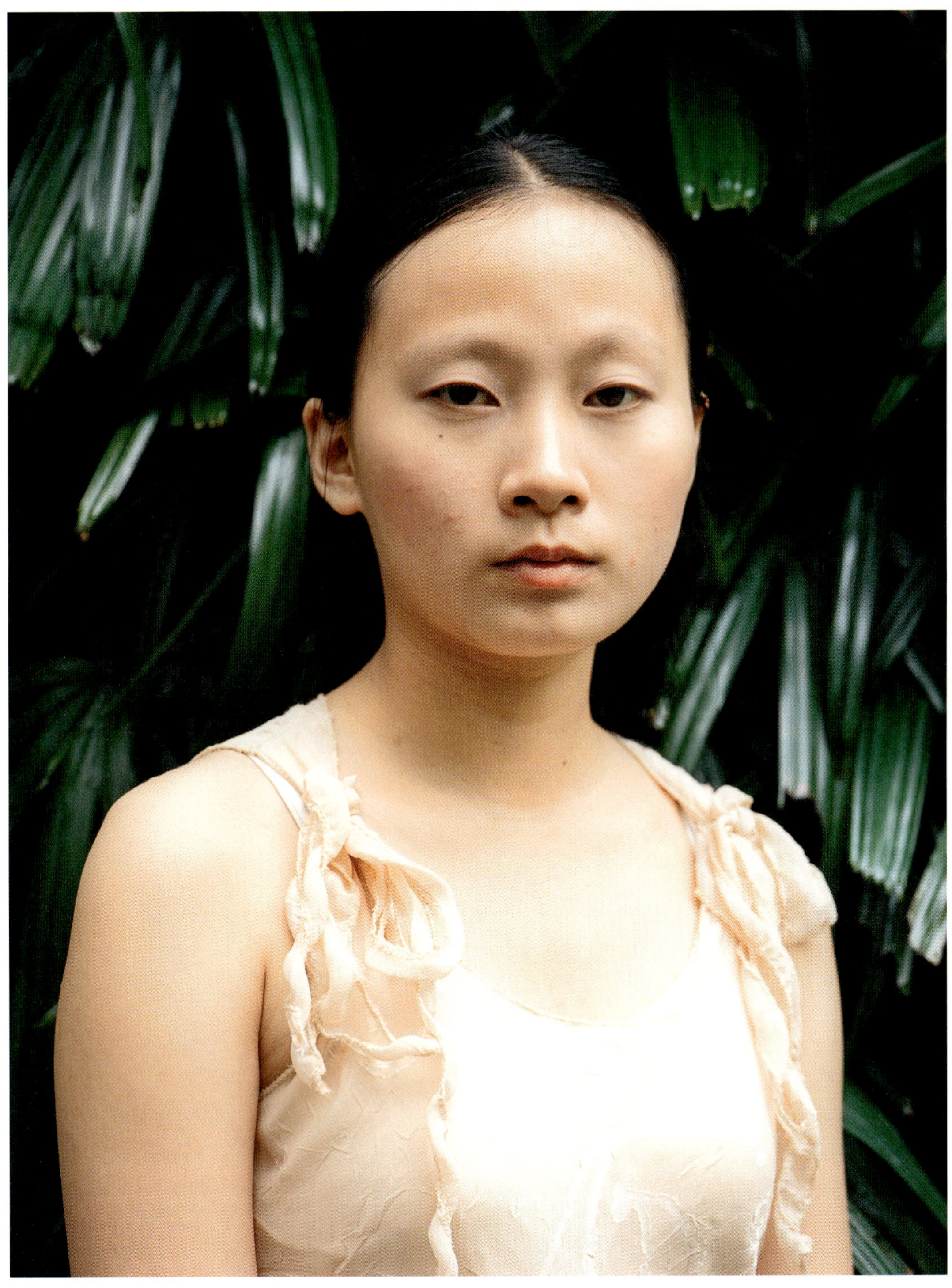

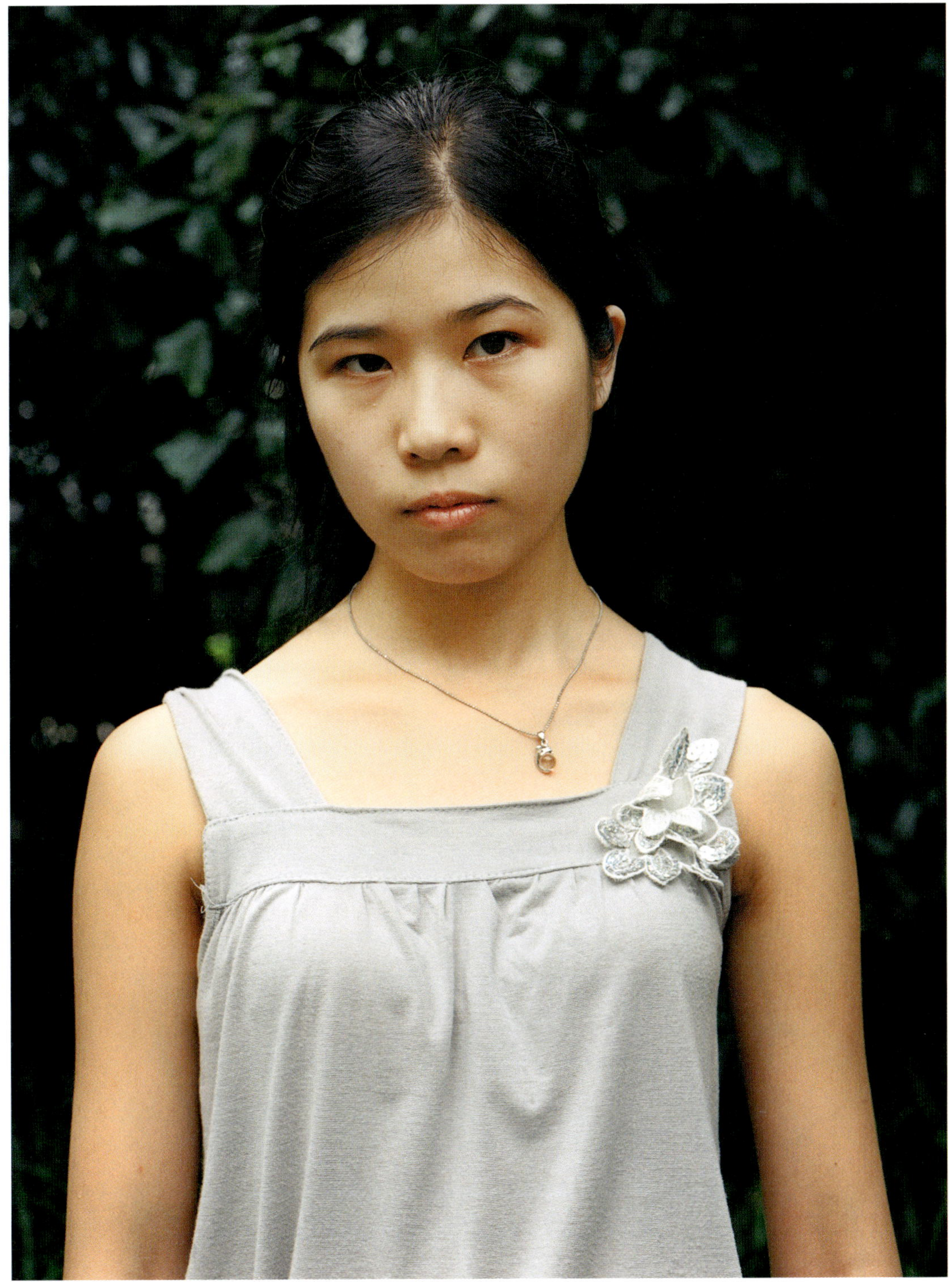

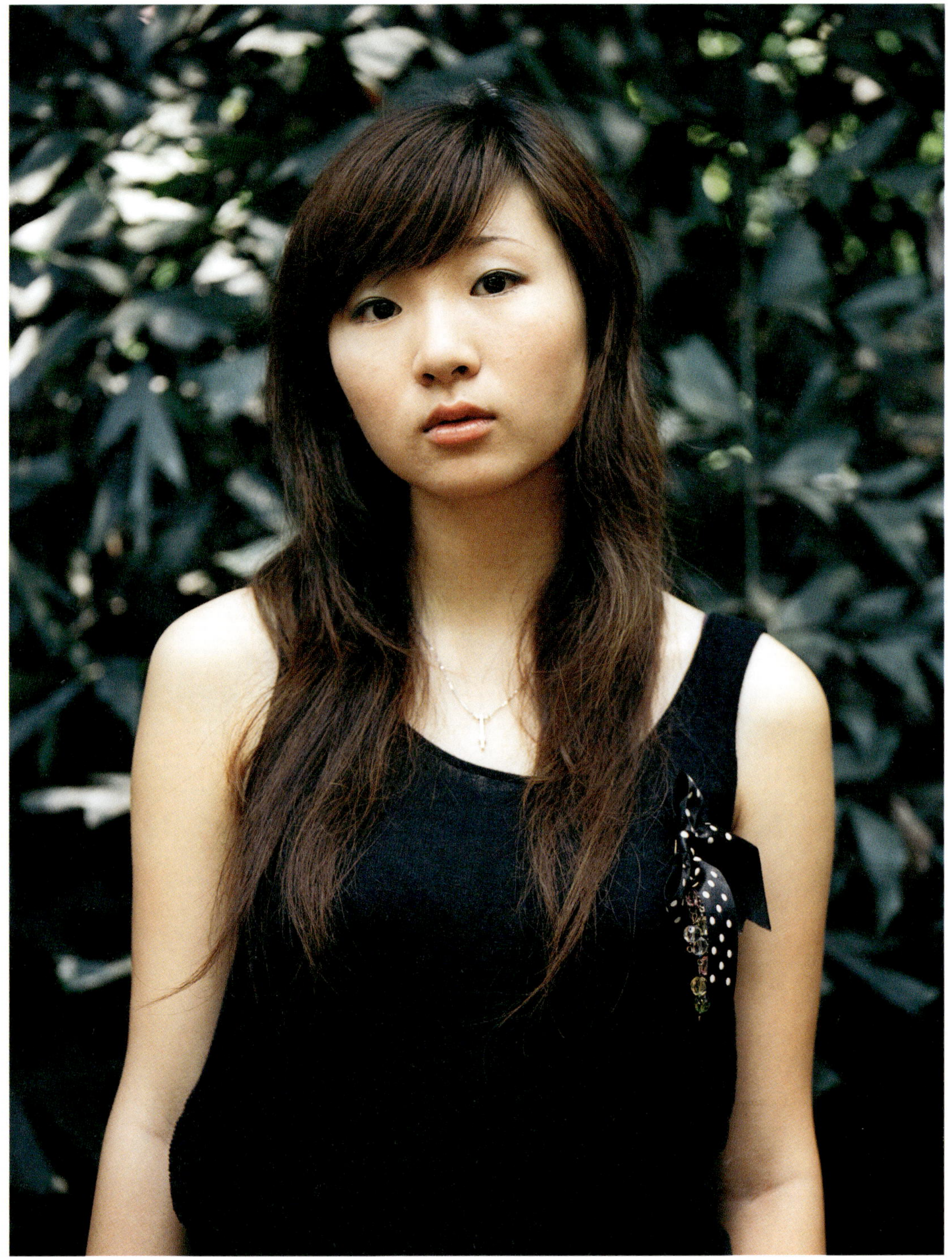

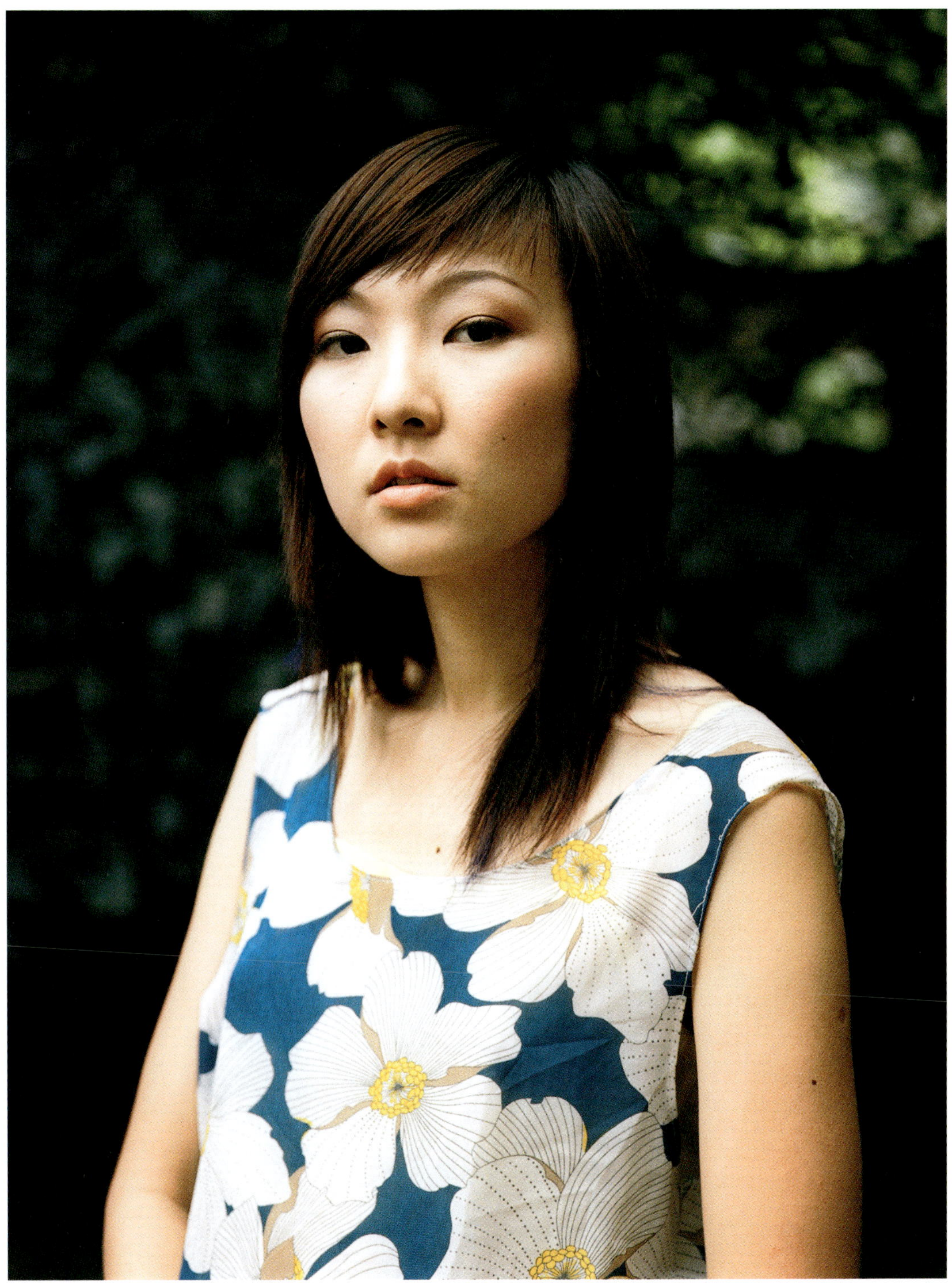

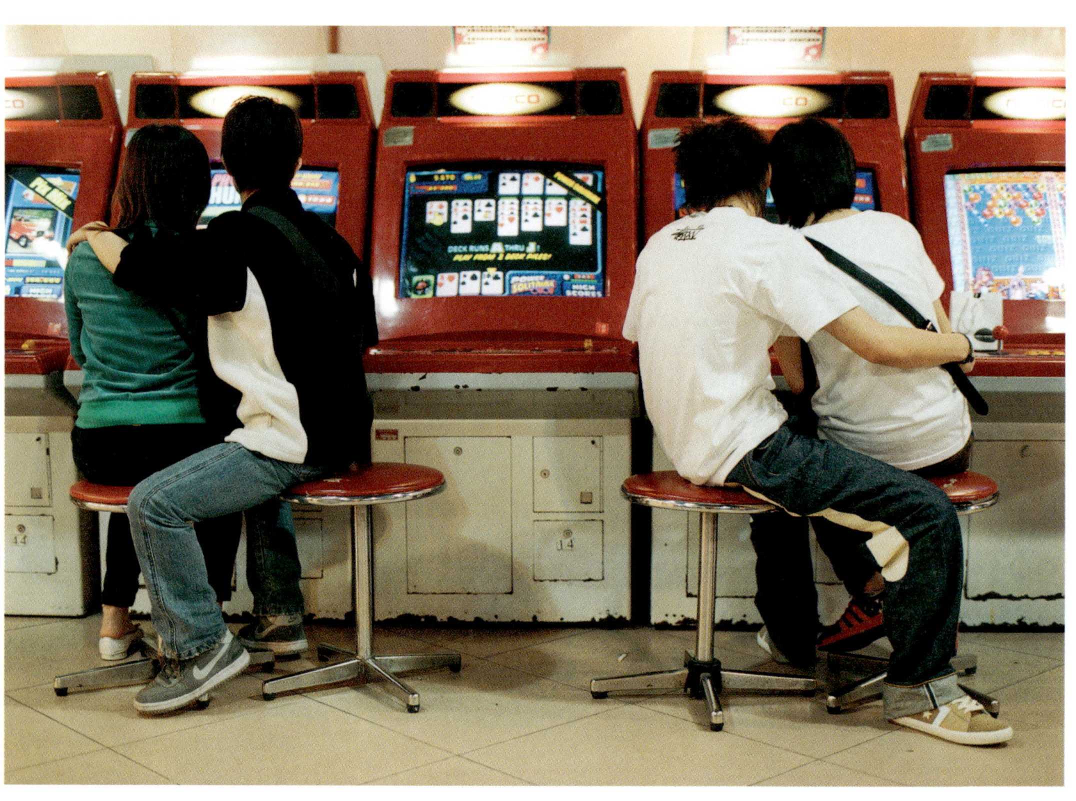

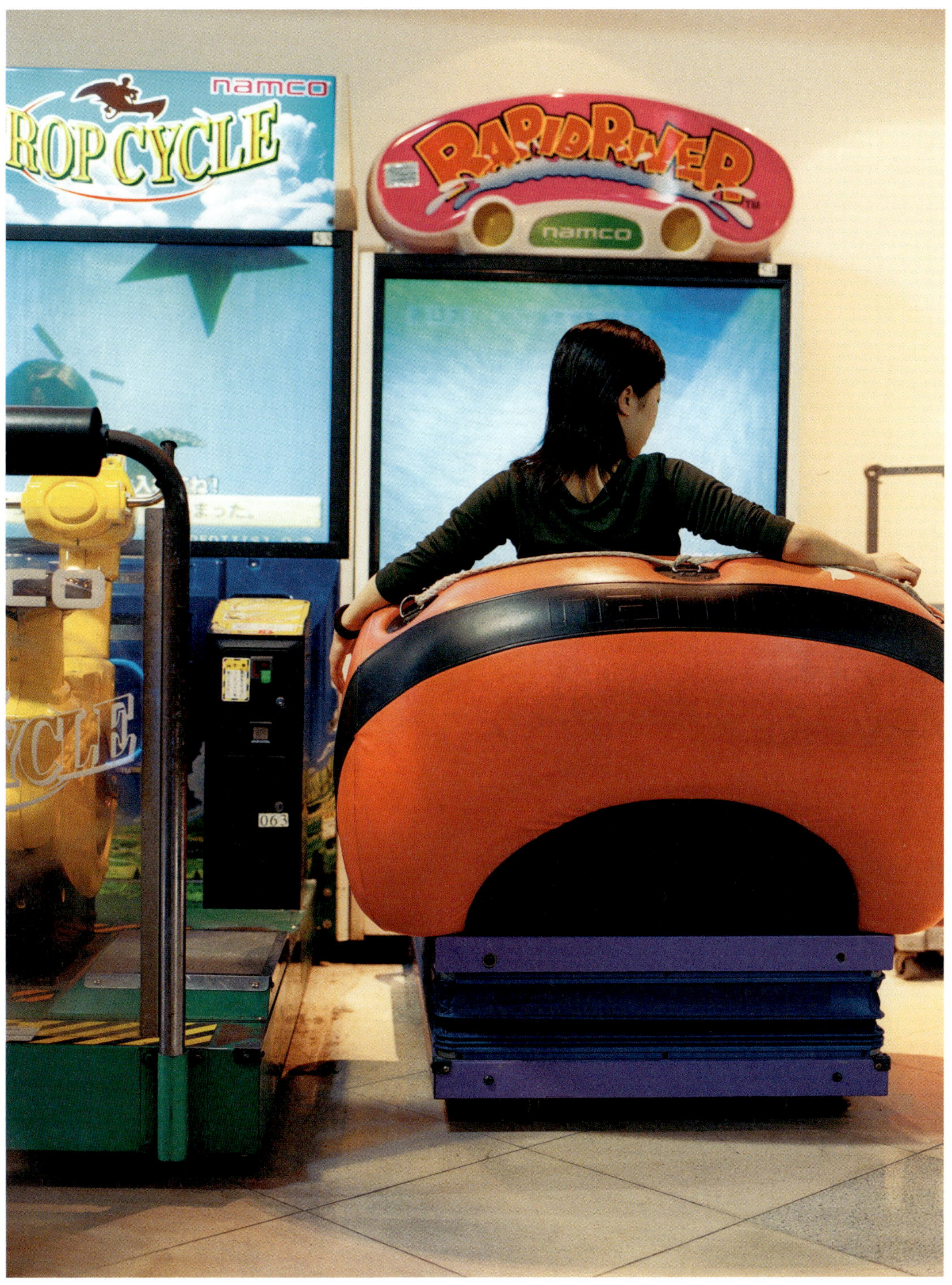
namco
DROP CYCLE
RAPID RIVER
namco
CYCLE
063

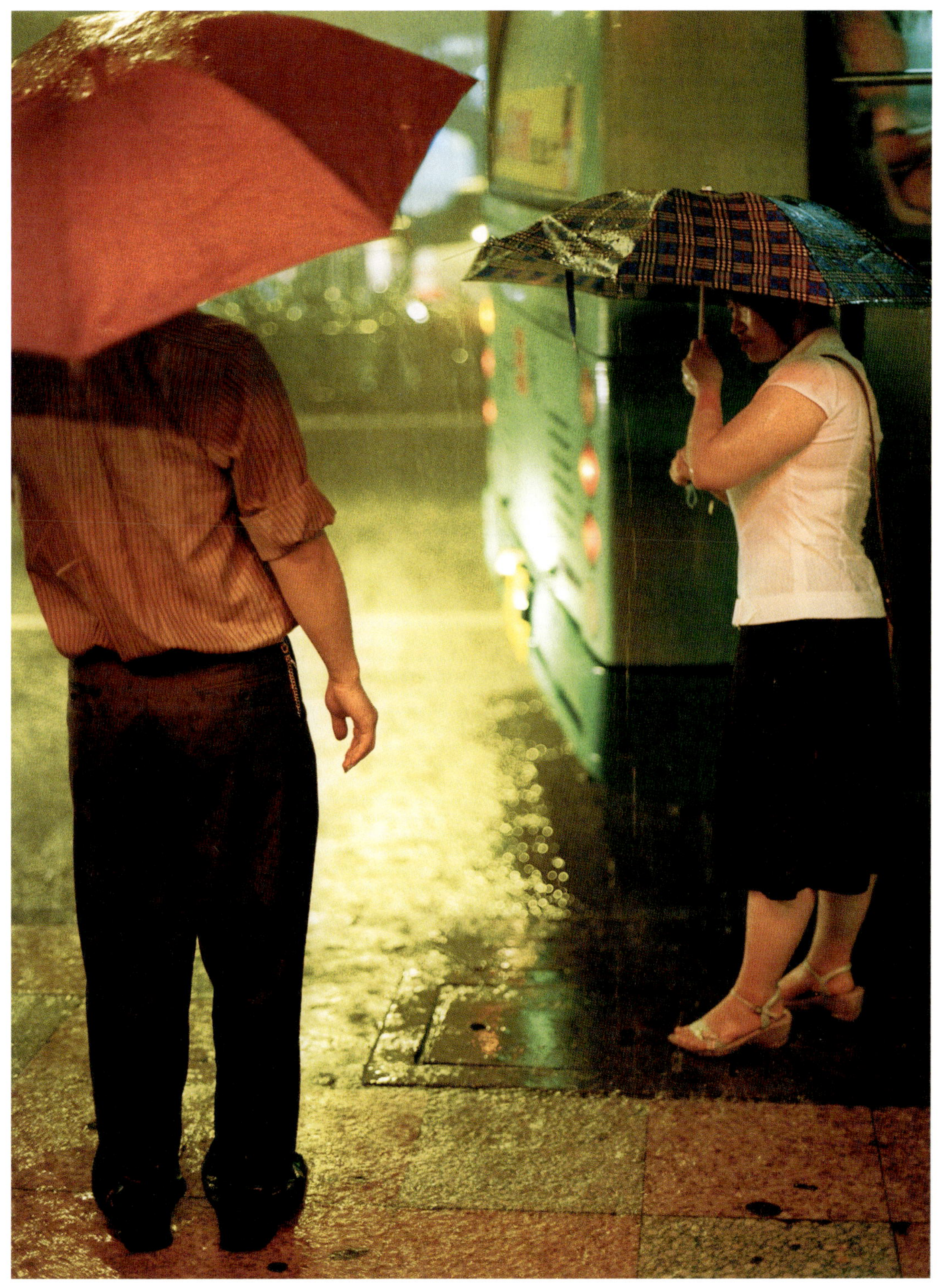

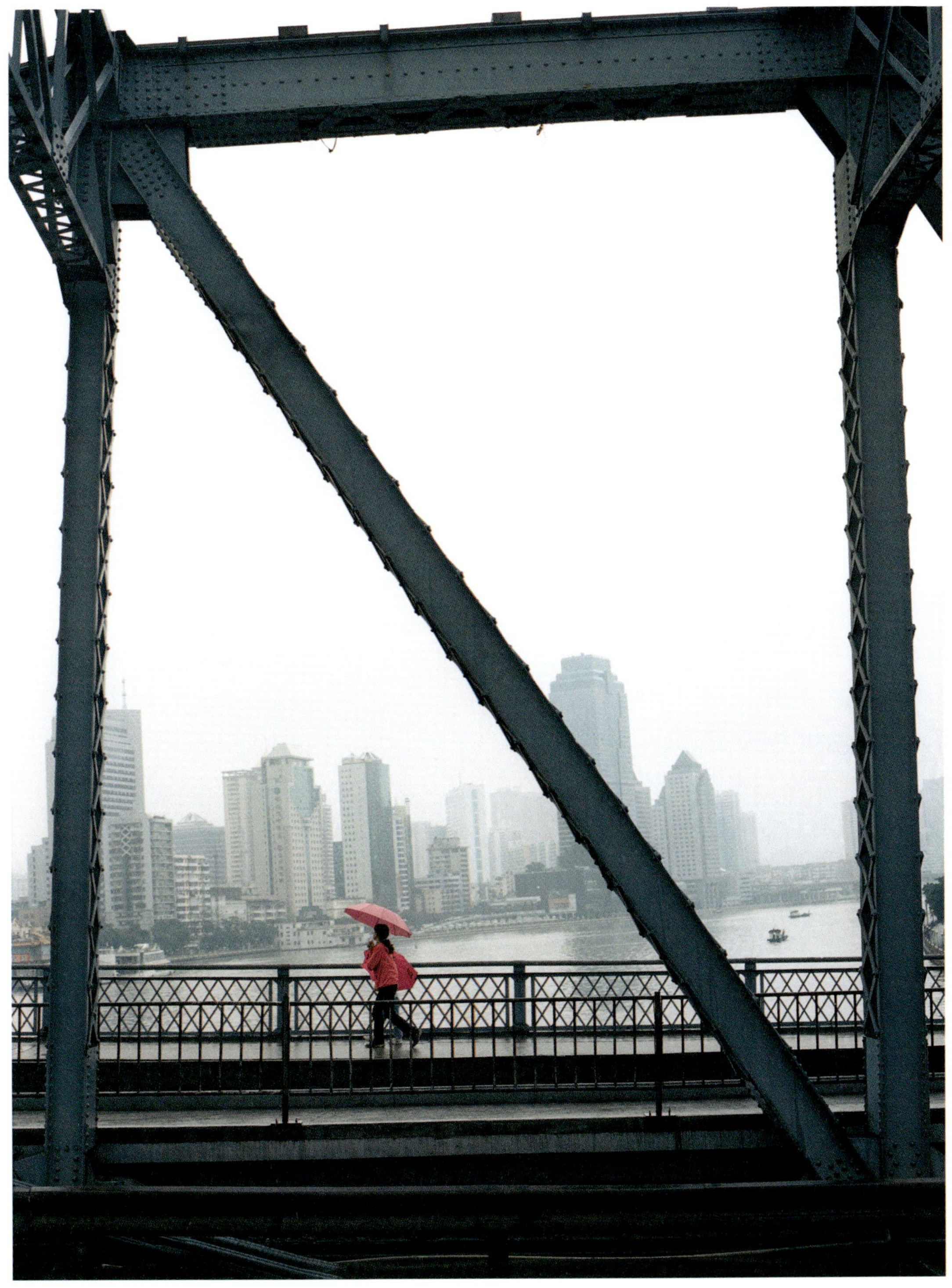

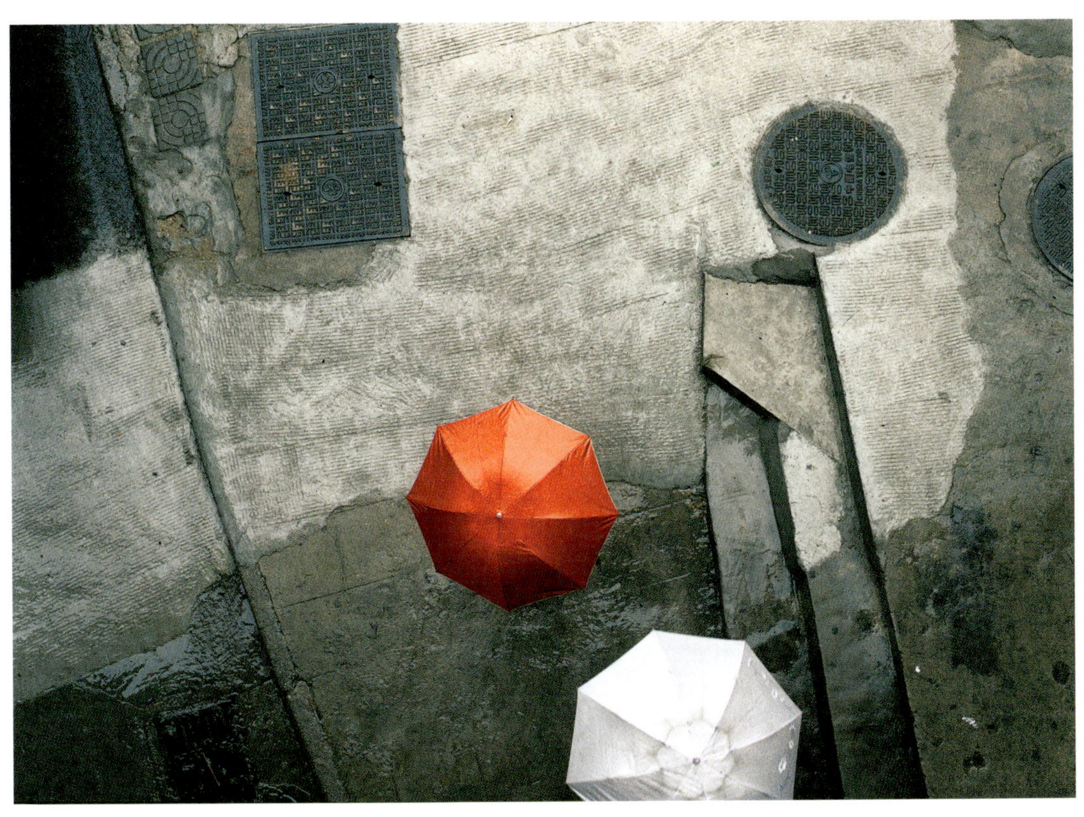

BETEL NUT BEAUTIES

TAIWAN 2006

The betel nut is a stimulant, comparable with caffeine and nicotine, that is commonly consumed in Southeast Asian countries. In Taiwan, consumption of betel nuts is extremely popular and gave rise in the 1990s to a unique phenomenon: Bin Lang Xishi, or, in English, the betel nut beauty. These girls got their name from Xi Shi, the daughter of a tea-merchant who according to legend was one of the most beautiful women China has ever known. She had a beauty that was so enchanting that it could bring down a corrupt empire.

The betel nut beauties nowadays use their beauty primarily to sell their product. On the outskirts of Taiwanese cities, at strategic places such as highway entrances, young women sit in glass kiosks, surrounded by colorful neon and flashing lights, preparing and selling small boxes of betel nuts. The women are often scantily clad to attract the attention of the mostly male clientele.

It has led to heated debates in Taiwan: are betel nut beauties a sign of moral decay in society or do they represent a woman's right to express and support herself? Is the attempt by local governments to regulate the betel nut beauties a sign of repression of individual rights? It remains a touchy subject in Taiwanese society, but while critics often place emphasis on negative aspects of the betel nut beauties, in recent years an independent generation of betel nut beauties has come to the fore: women who started selling betel nuts at an early age for someone else, but now manage their own kiosk.

The fashion of betel nut beauties is sexy and provocative for some, but at the same time it reflects youth culture as it is seen in the shopping districts of Taipei, the popular Japanese Manga-comic strips, and in the pop-culture media. Their connection with the legendary Xi Shi is well chosen. In their modern world of asphalt and neon lights, it is unlikely that the betel nut beauties will bring down an empire, but their glaring position in the marketplace represents a self-conscious and independent assault against old barriers.

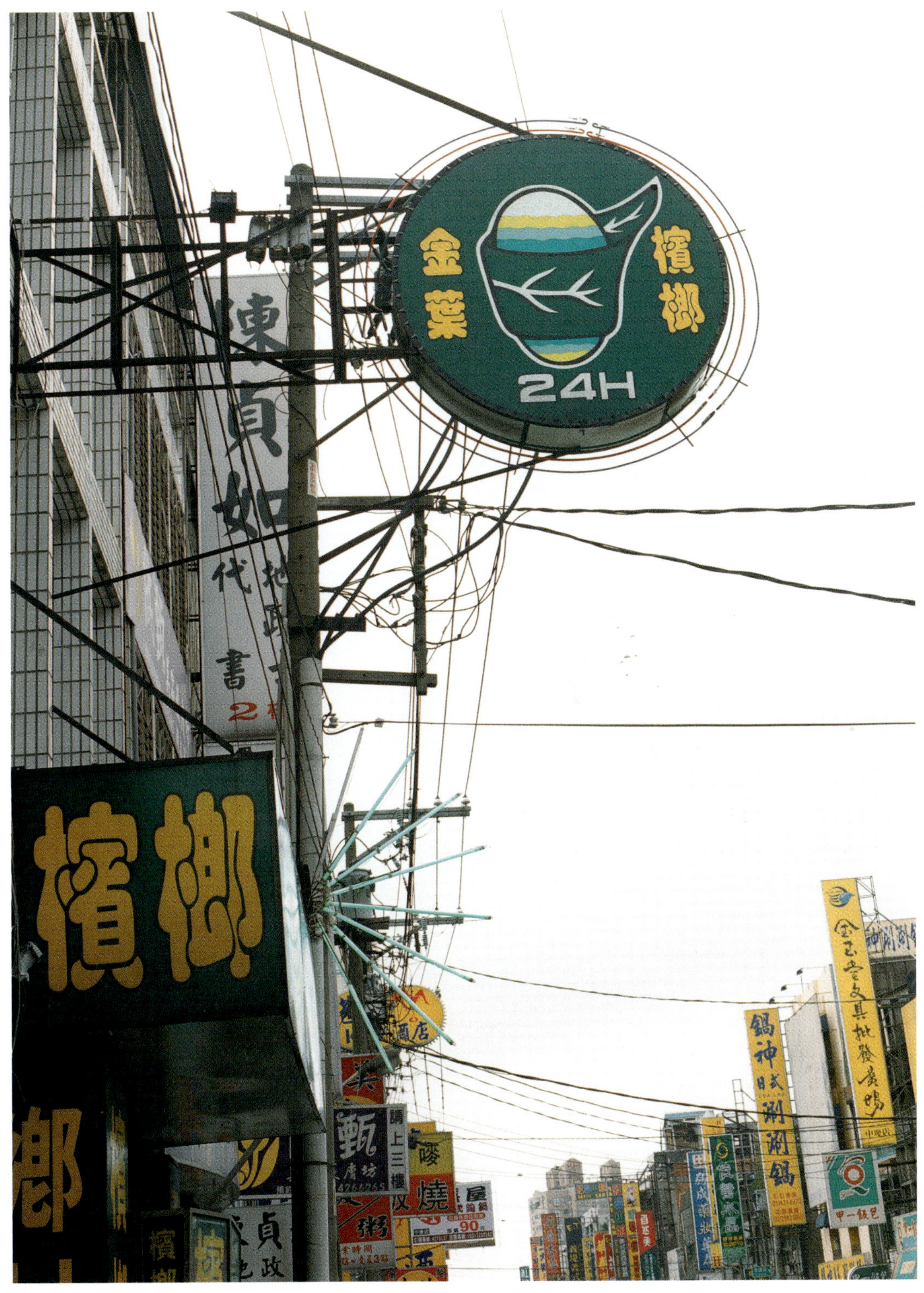

金葉
檳榔
24H
檳榔
郎

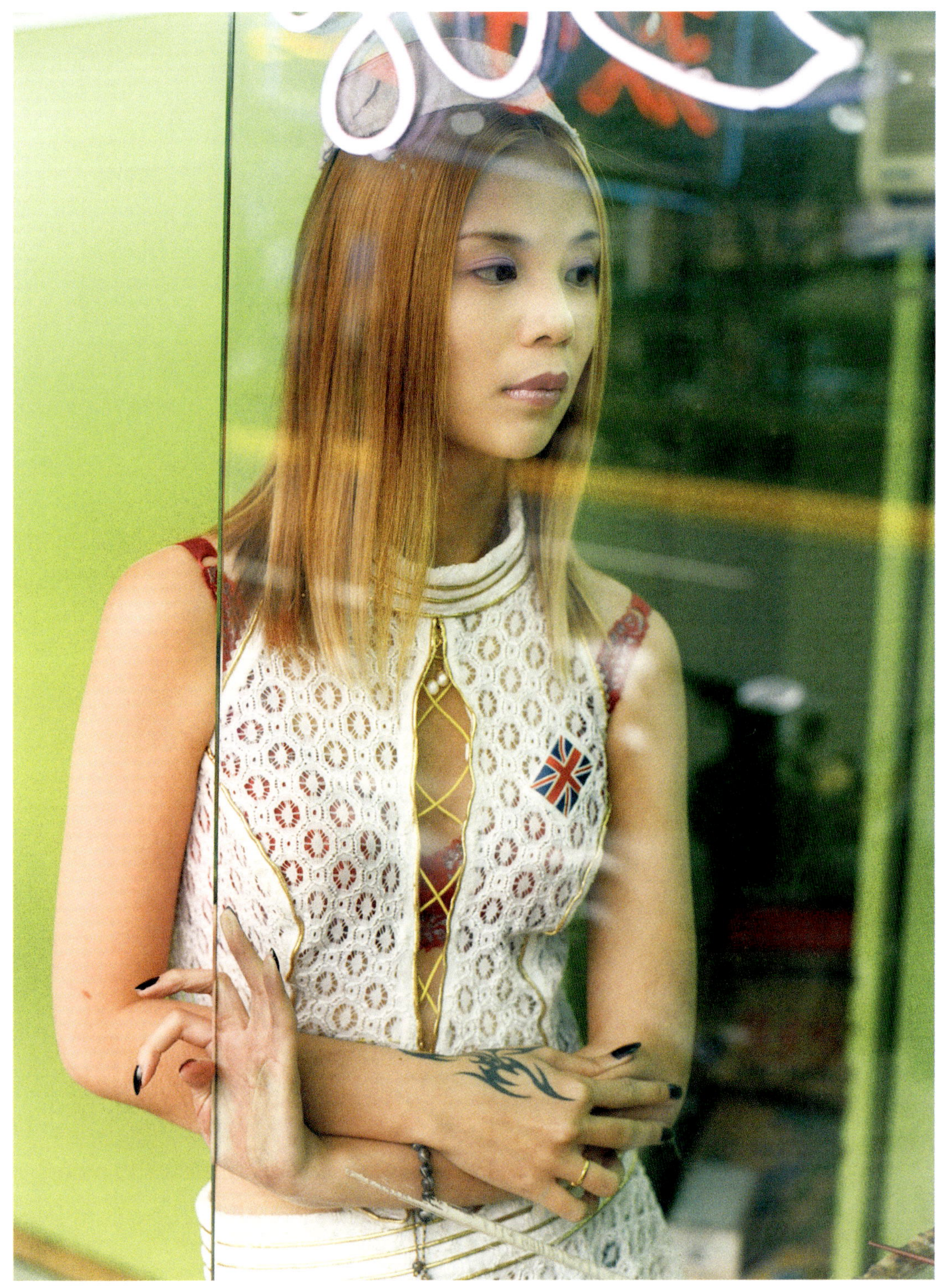

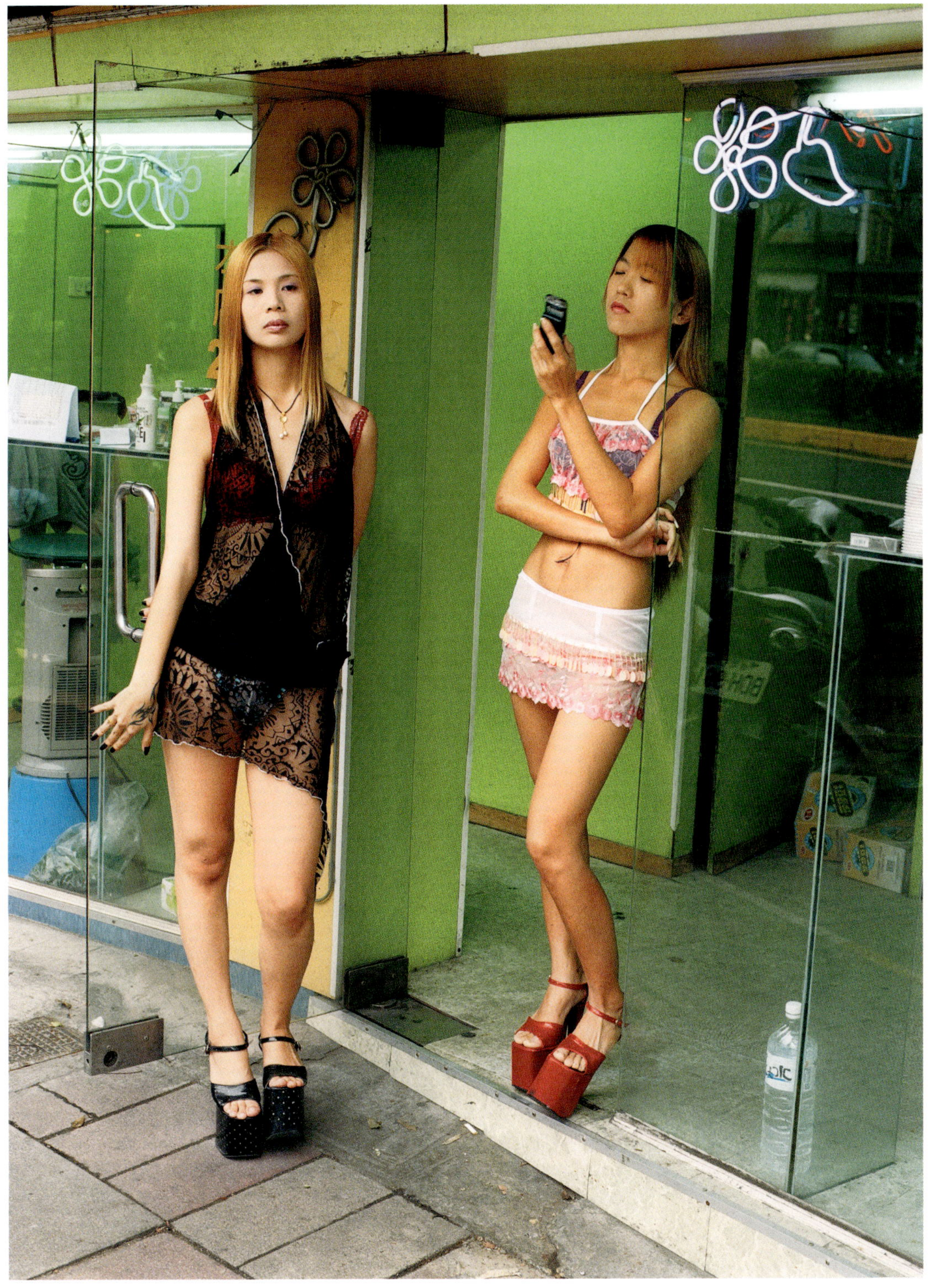

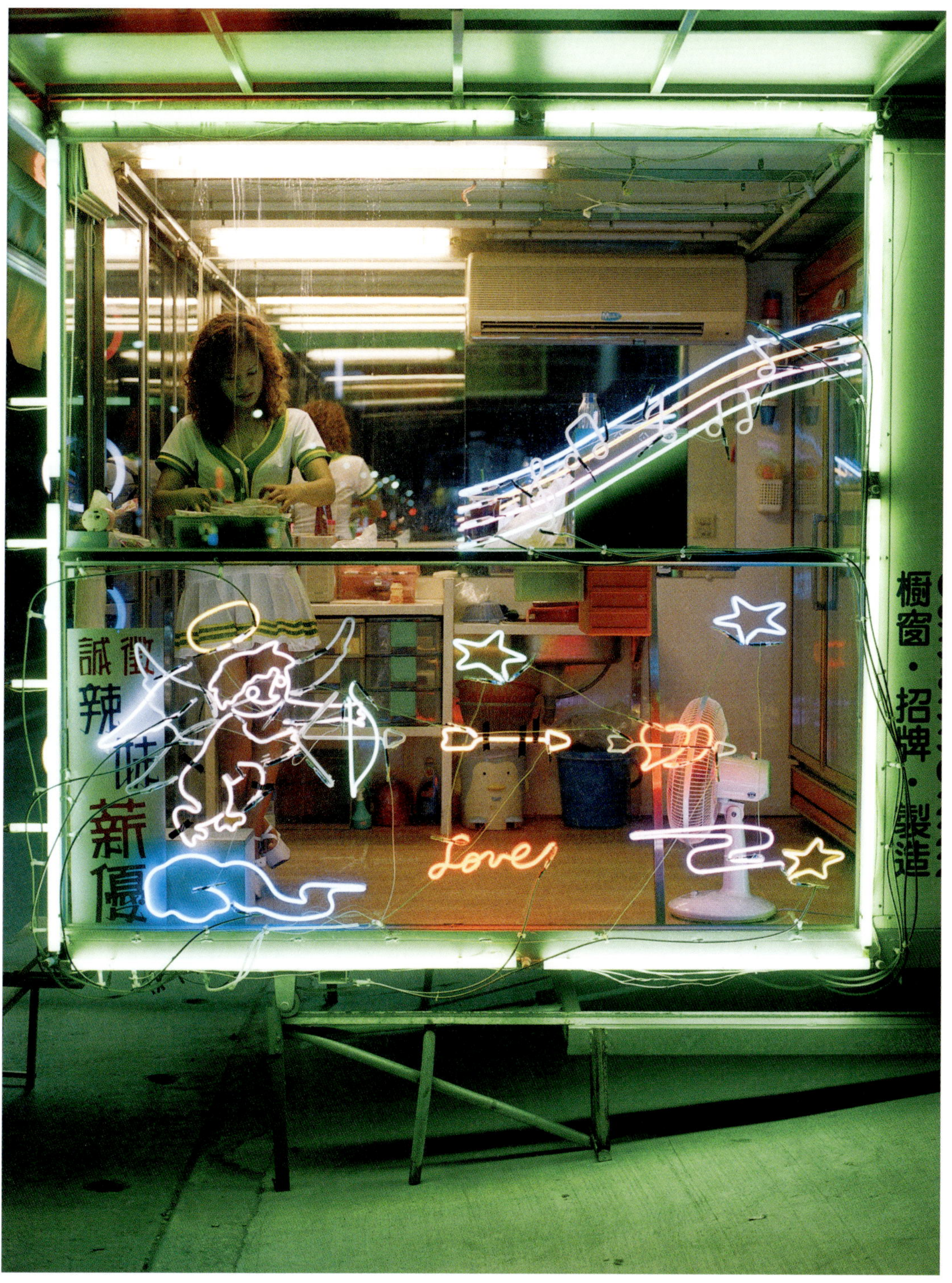
誠徵
辣妹
薪優
Love
櫥窗・招牌・製造

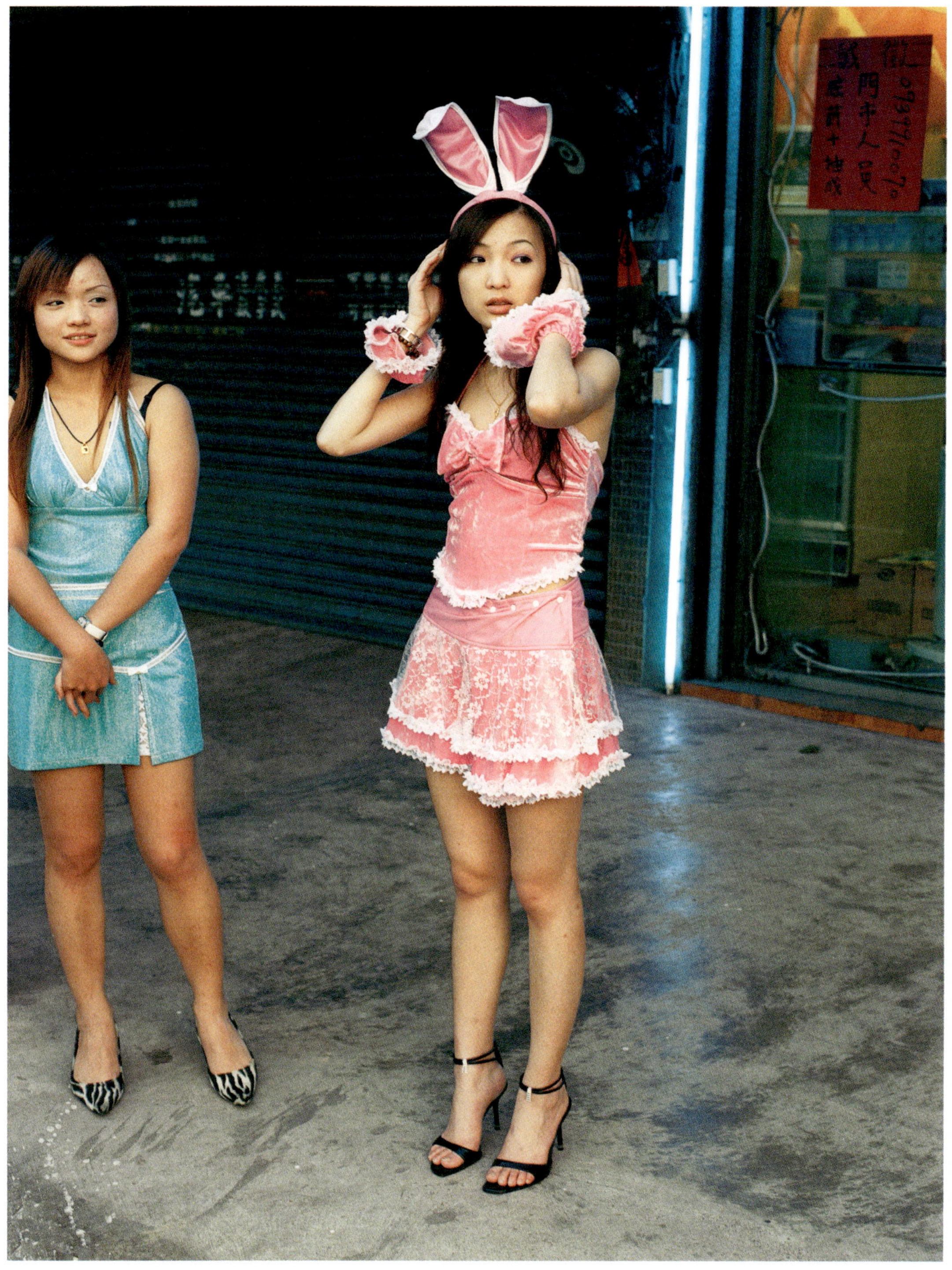
微_o9397(oo7o
門市人員
試底薪+抽成

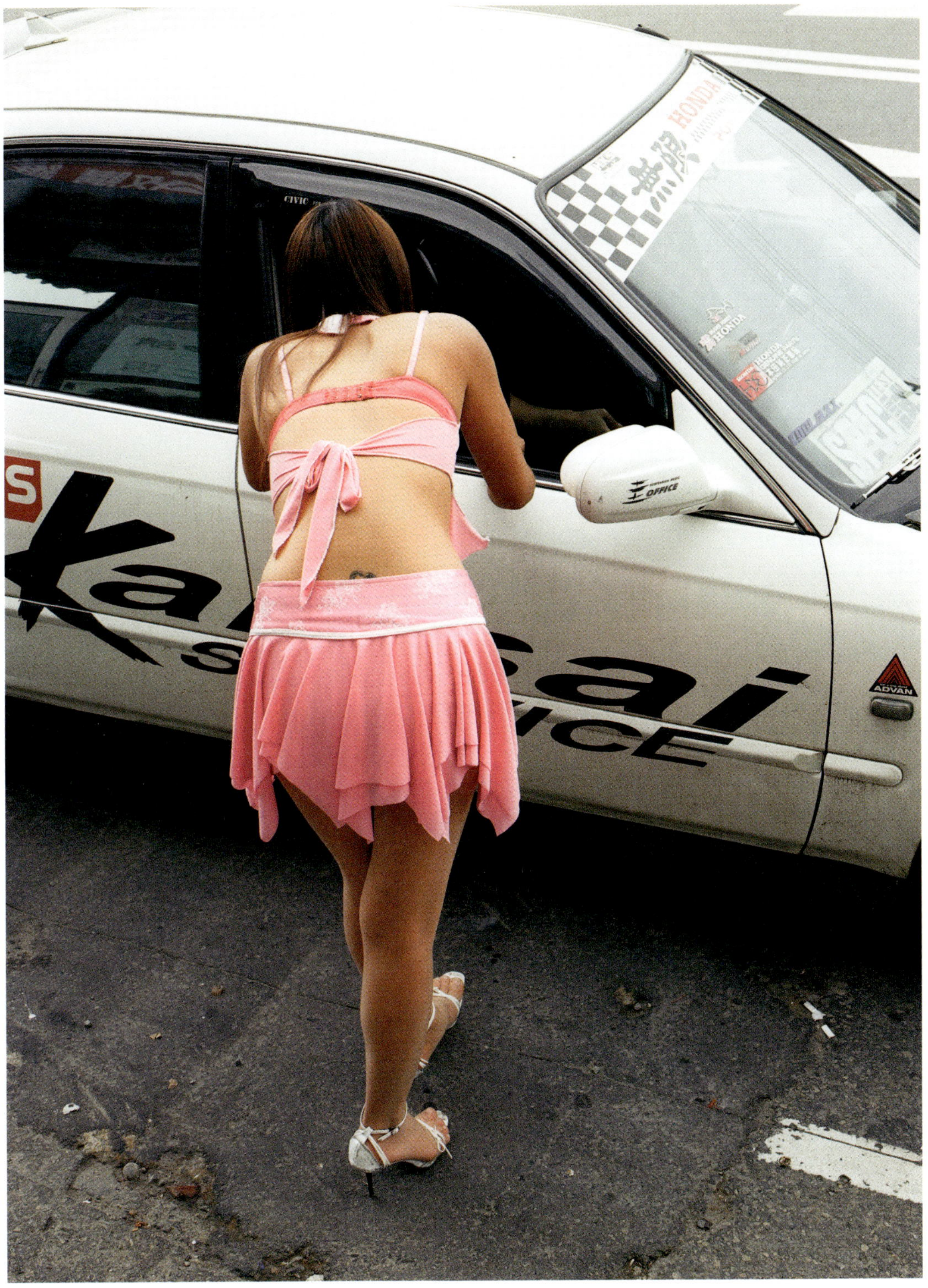

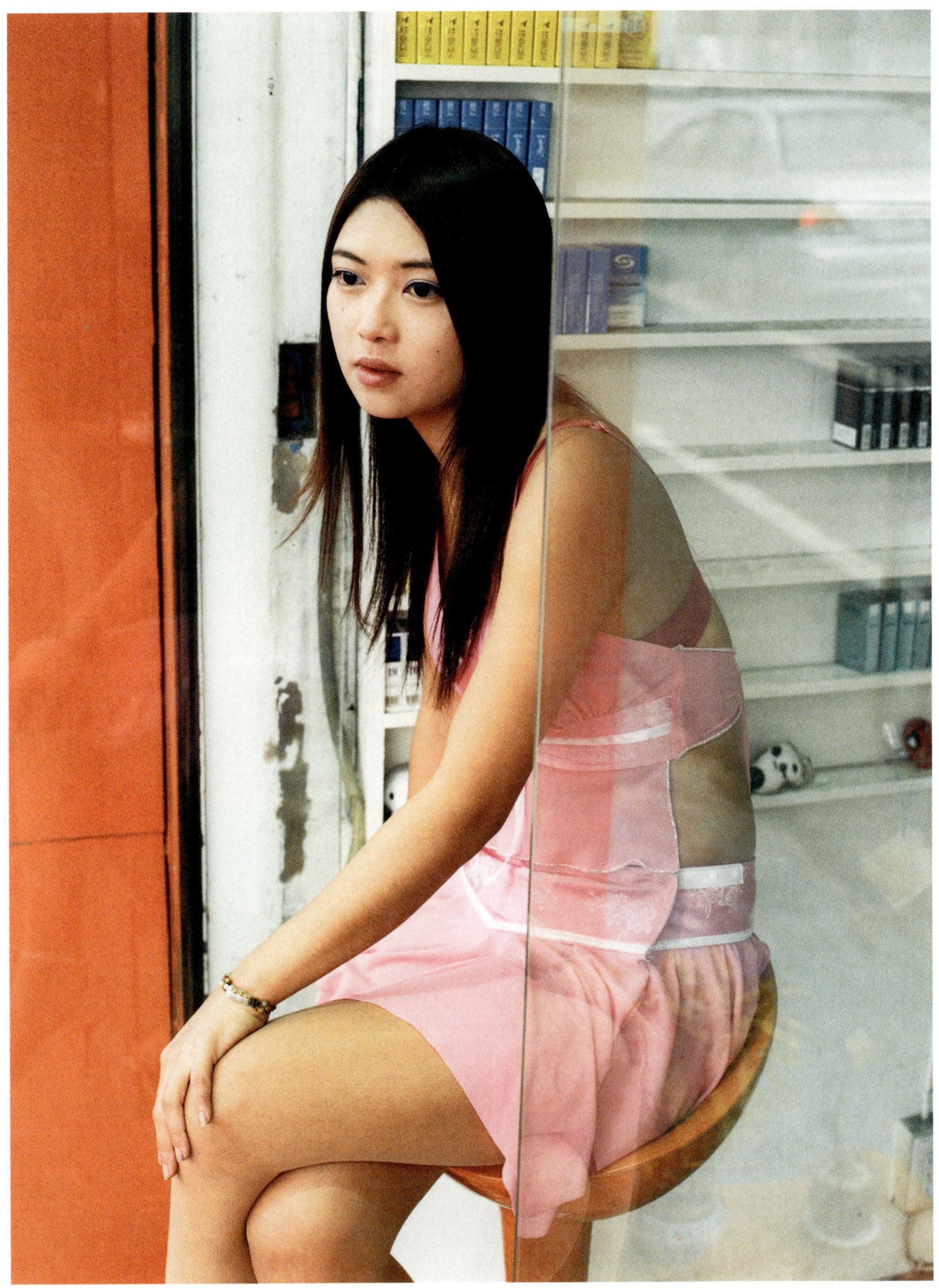

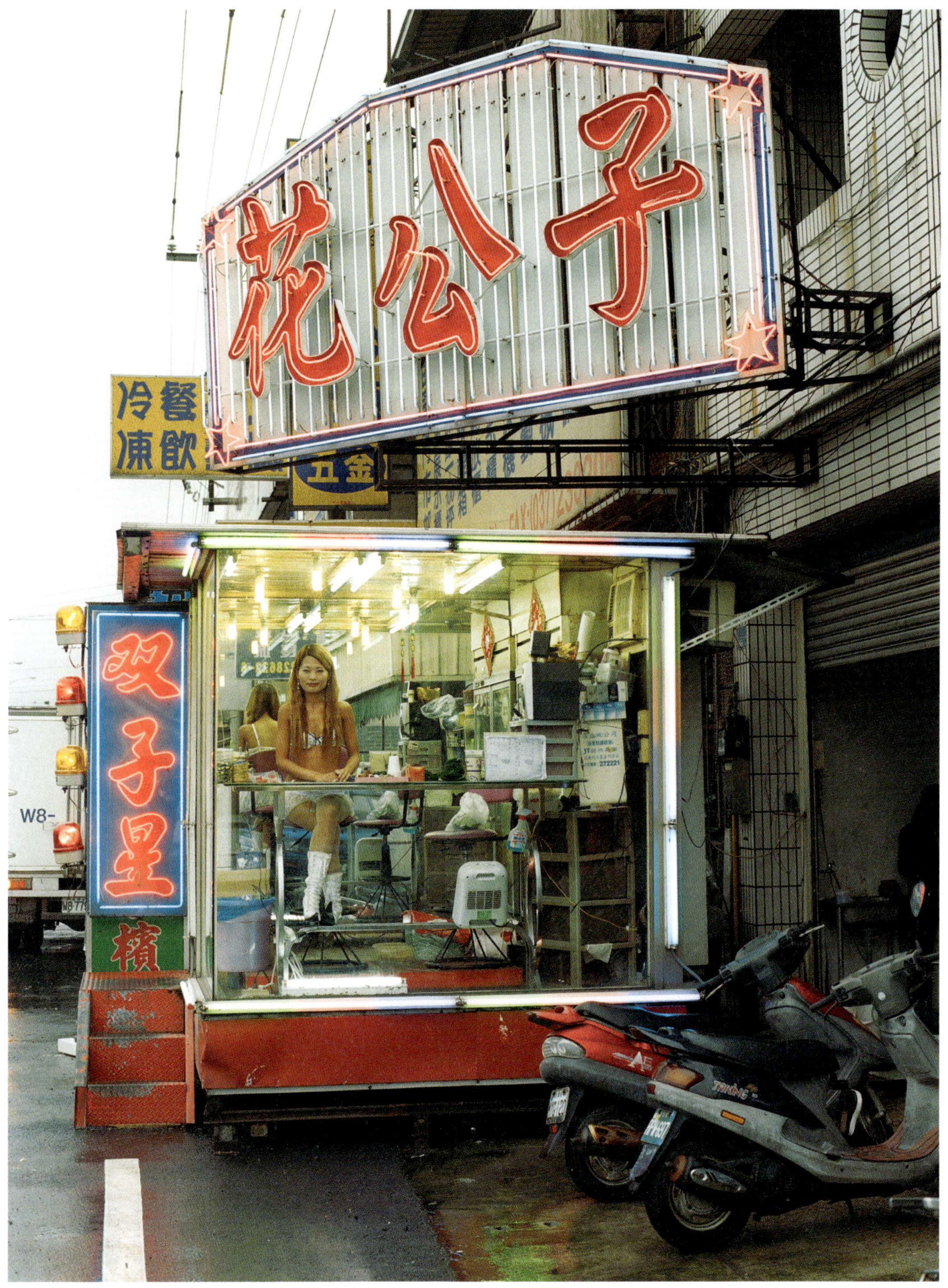
花公子
子公花
冷餐
凍飲
五金
雙子星
檳

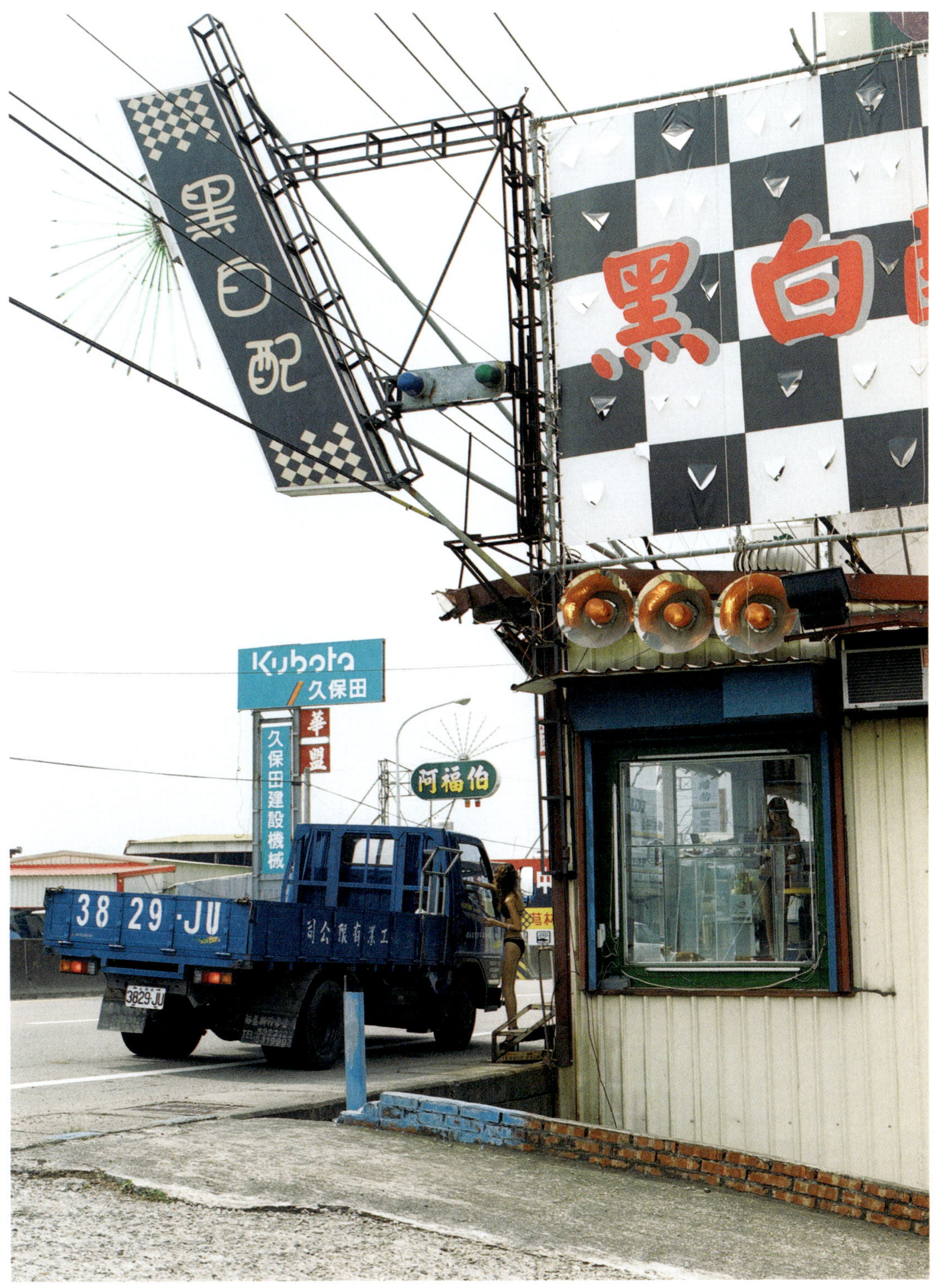

黑白配
黑白配
Kubota
久保田
久保田建設機械
華盟
阿福伯
38 29·JU
司公機有業工
3829·JU

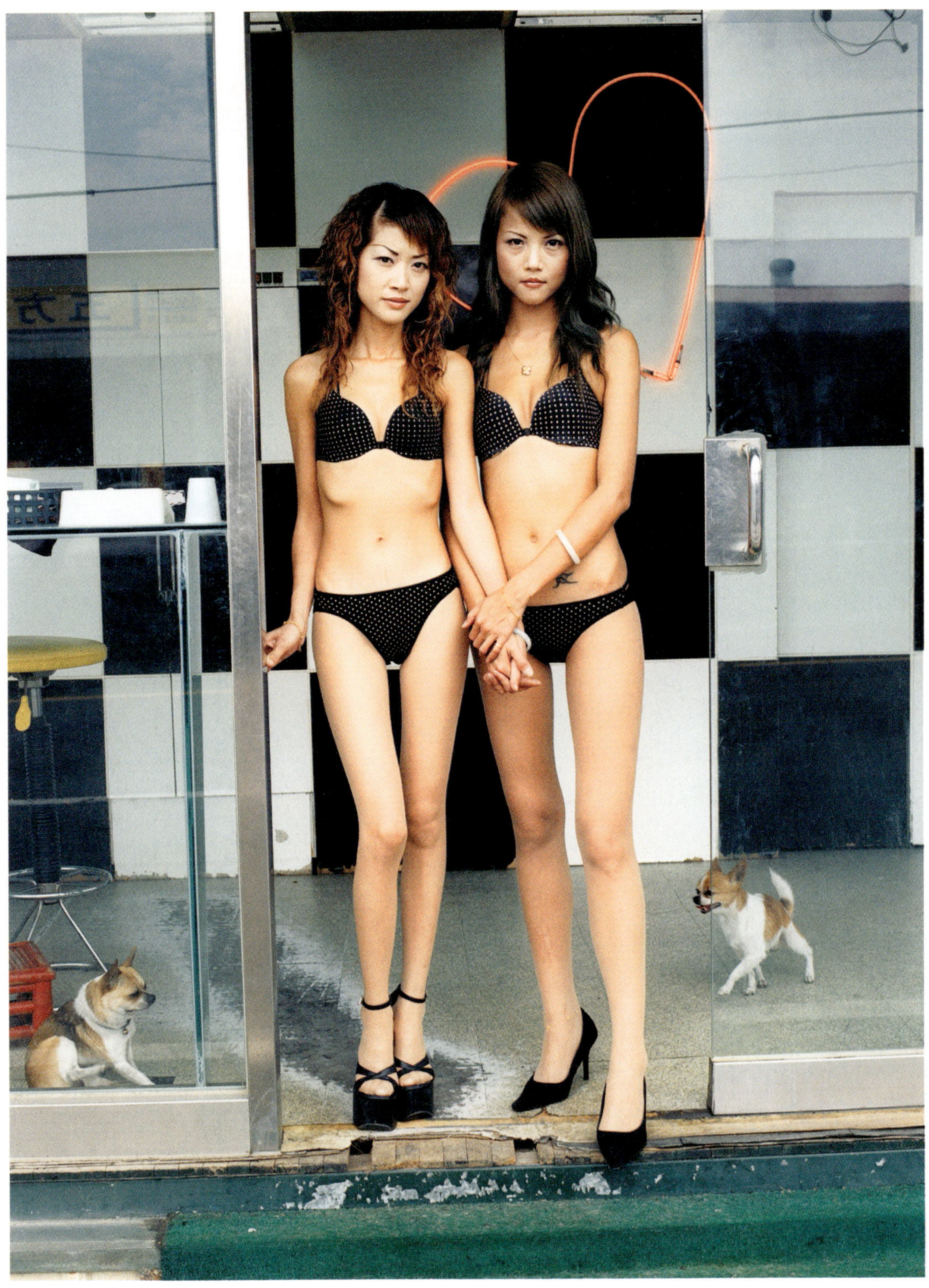

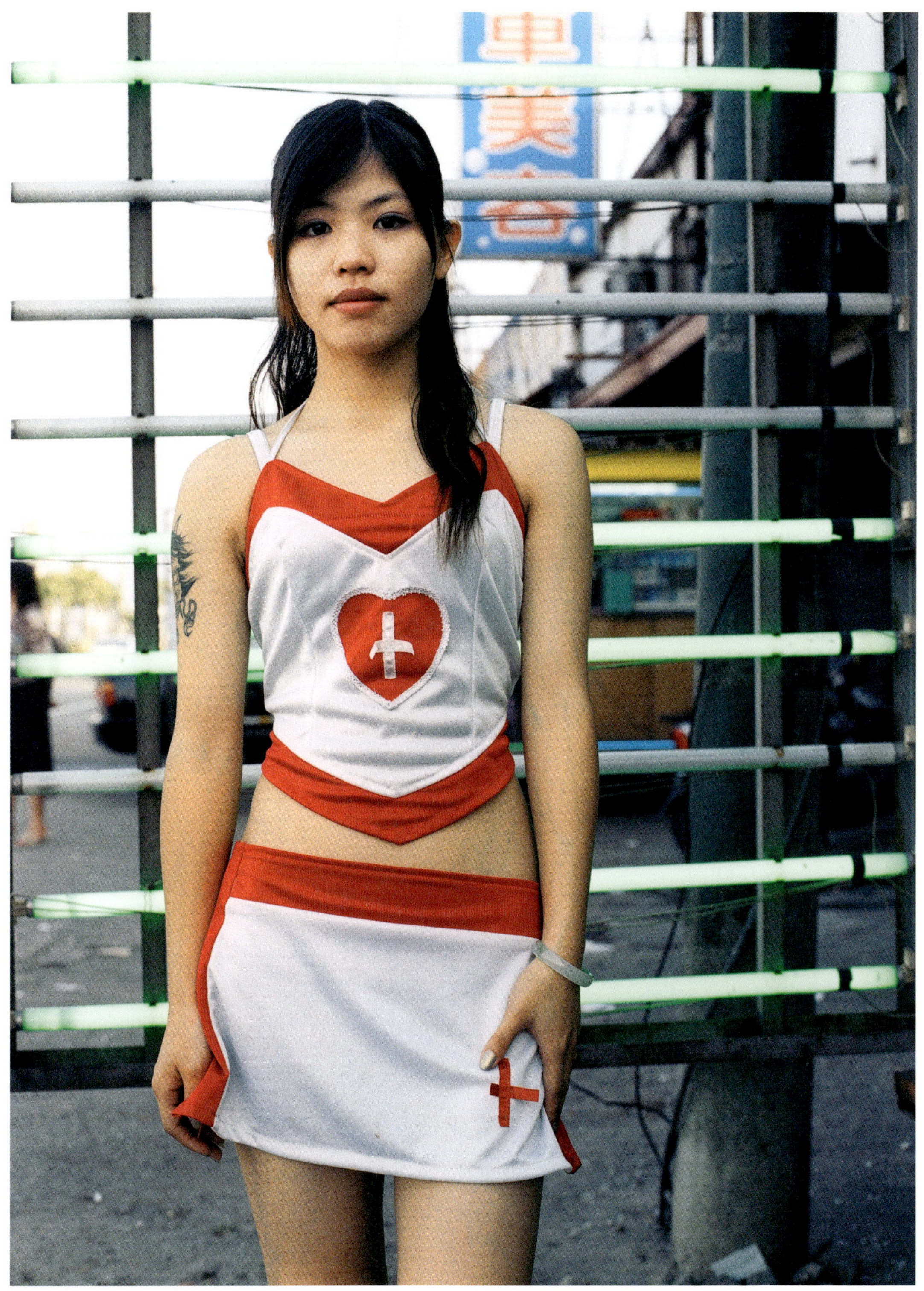
串
美
合

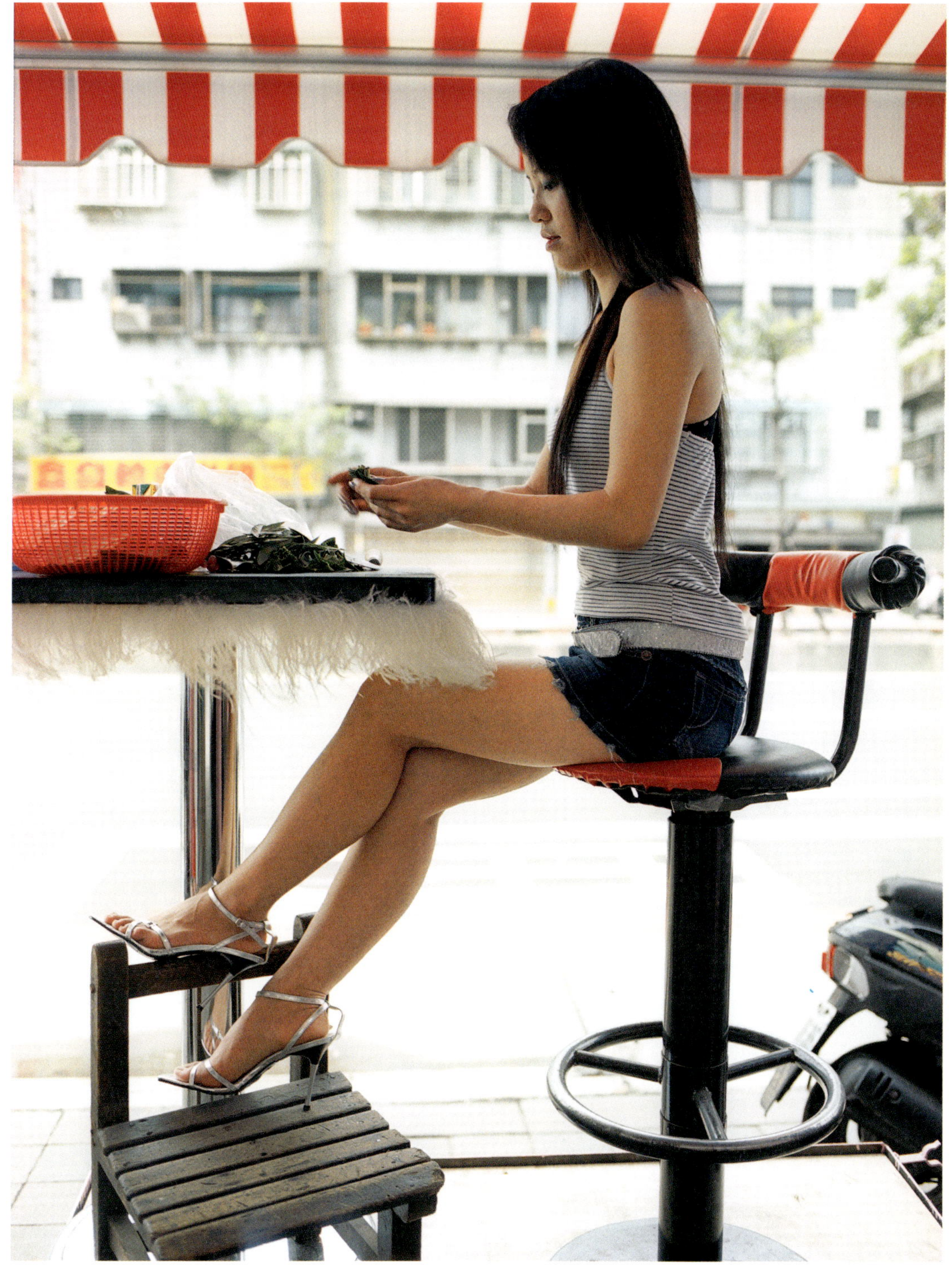

HIGH SCHOOLS

SEOUL, SOUTH KOREA 2006

Uniformity fascinates me. In an attempt to create equality among people, at least in appearance, small details become more obvious, more enlarged. Individuality peeks through the surface no matter how uniformly people are dressed. In this way, uniformity emphasizes individuality.

Perhaps in contradiction to my earlier words, I am drawn as a photographer towards subjects in which uniformity plays a role. It does not matter much if it concerns coalminers or Buddhist monks, ballet dancers or high school kids. I like the tranquility that uniformity gives to an image, to a composition. I am fond of the order that uniformity lends to a photograph. I like the way small differences appear to form an expression: nail polish, a bit of make-up, MP3 players or the newest cell phone worn as modern jewelry.

During the project I also grew fascinated by the ways Korean schools use punishments and rewards. Physical punishments are doled out with ease—a twist of an ear or a slap on the back— while signs at the entrance of a classroom declare that the class is excellent in attendance or in keeping the classroom neat. At one school I found a girl sitting on the floor at the back of a classroom with a table on her head. She had to sit for an hour like that. It is an image that keeps haunting me. As a teenager I was difficult, at moments uncontrollable, and was punished and beaten by teachers fairly often. I see this girl and I imagine my teenage body crushed under all the tables of the school.

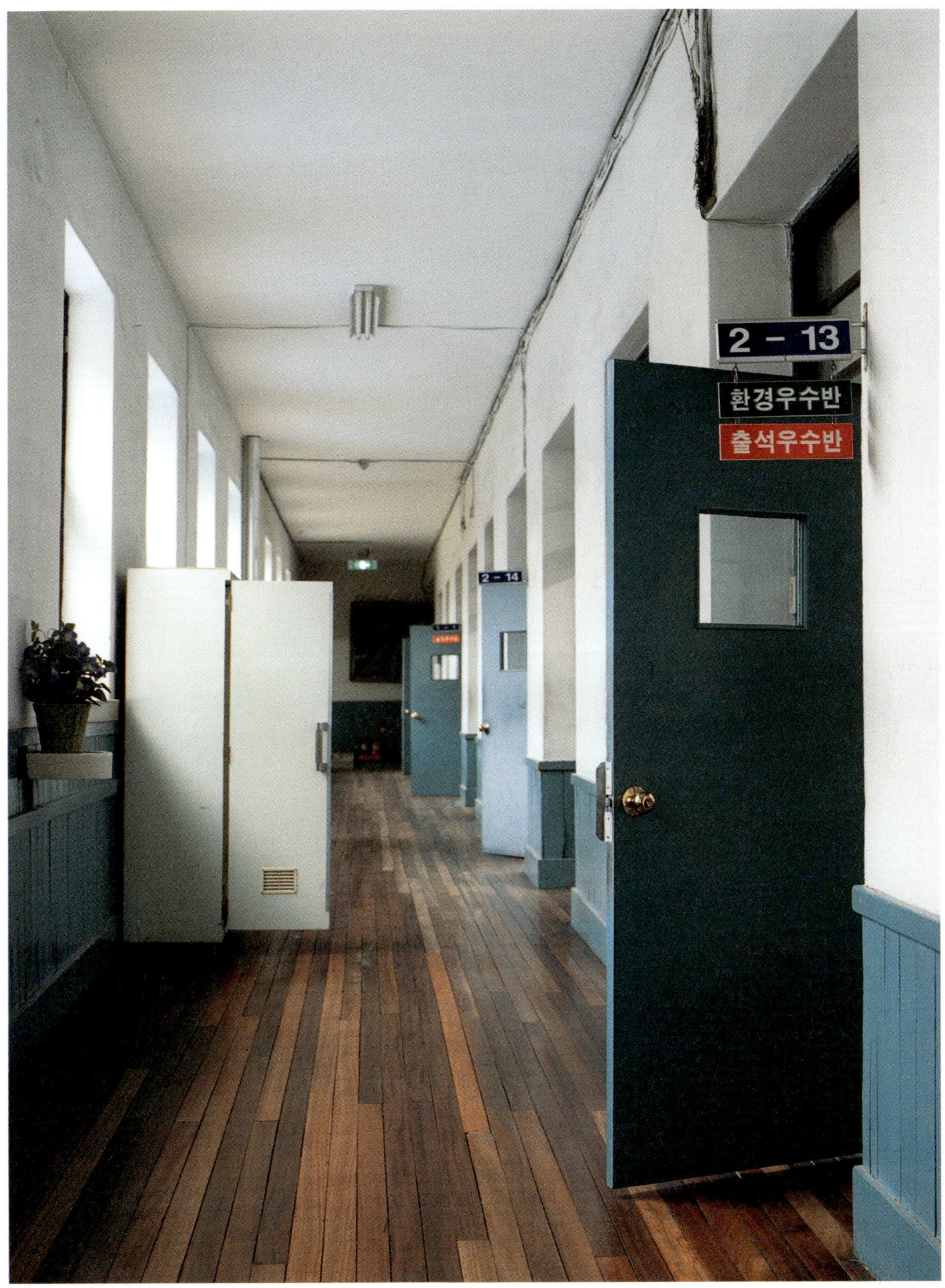
2 - 13
환경우수반
출석우수반
2 - 14

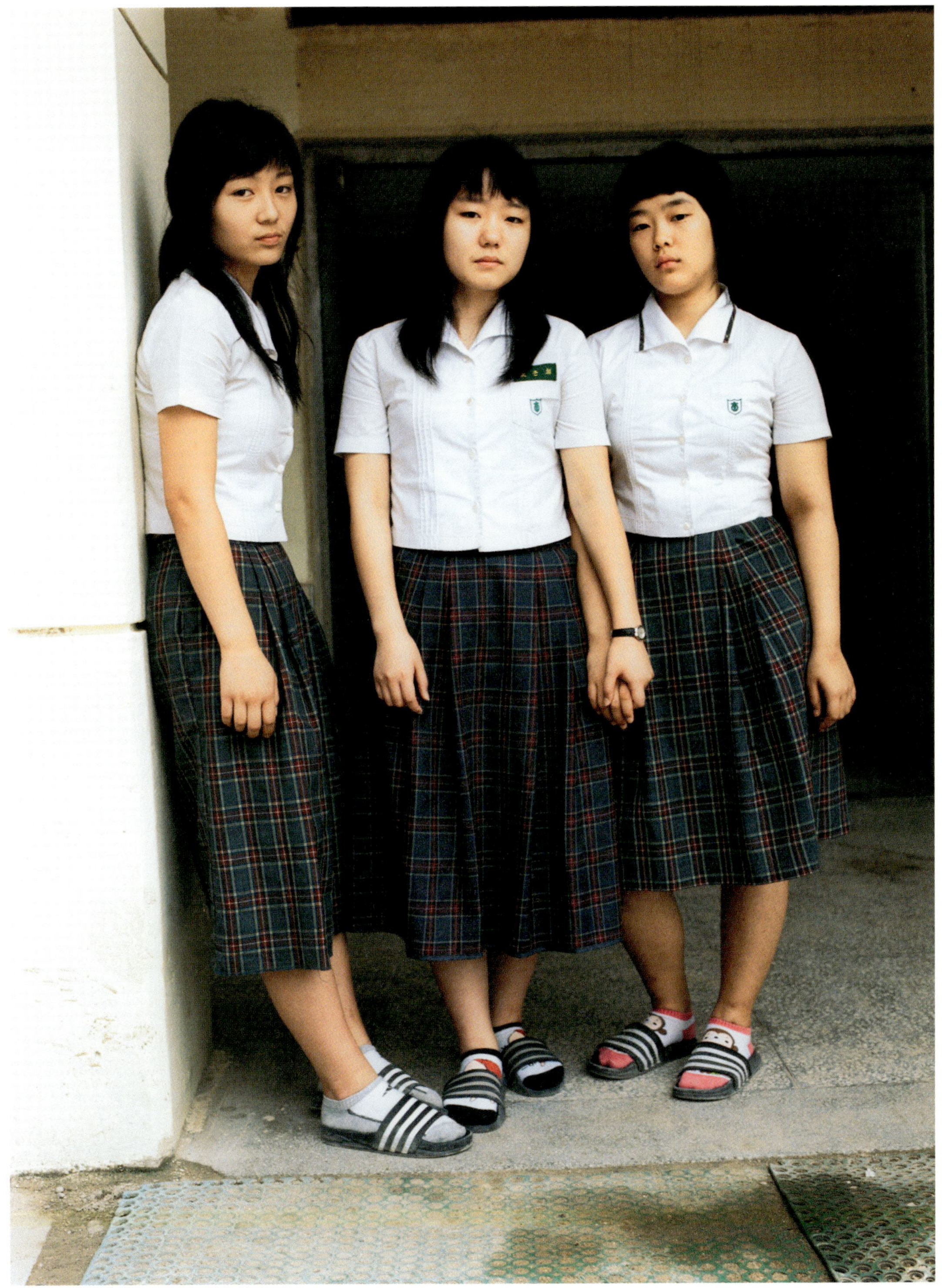

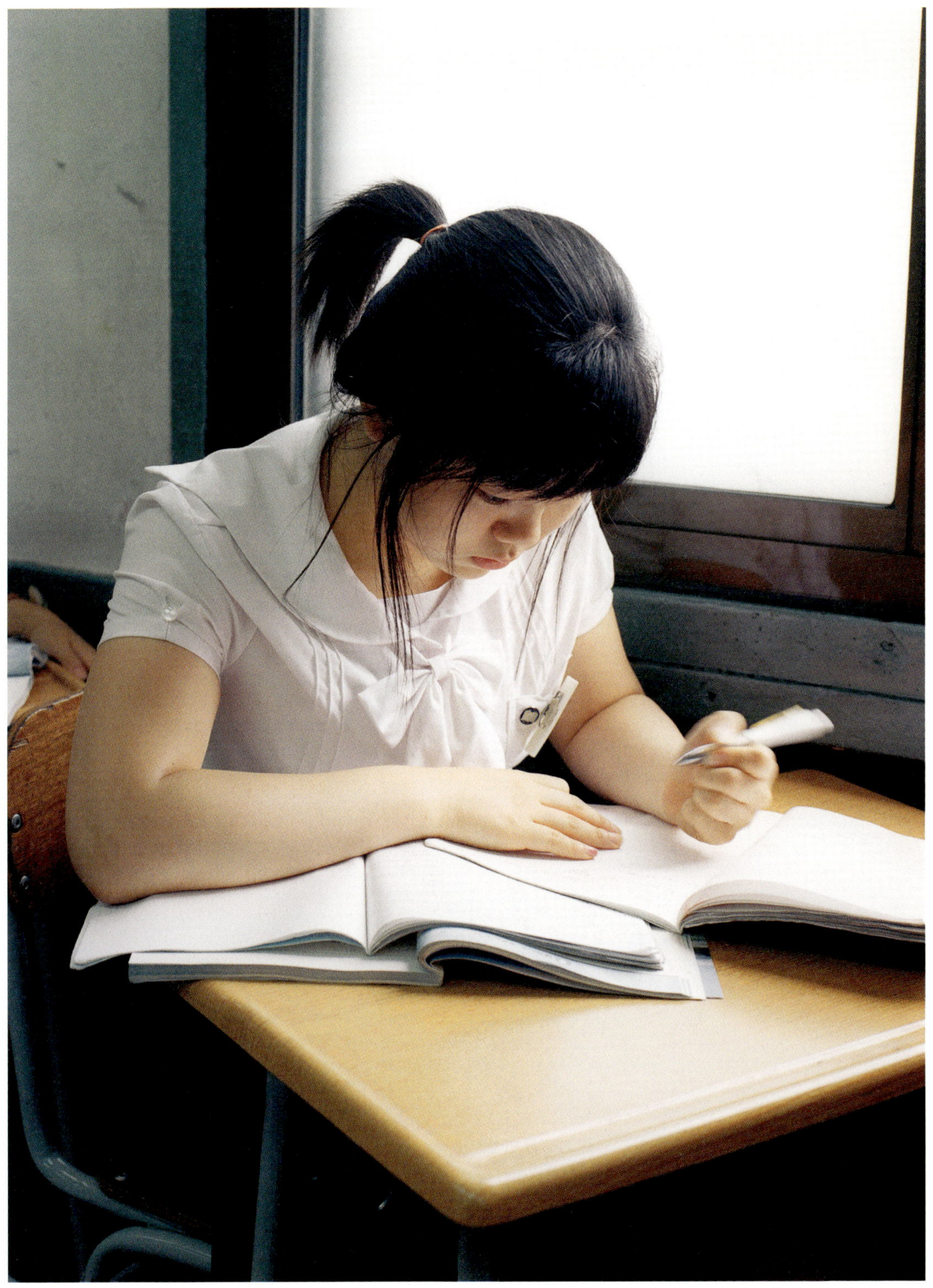

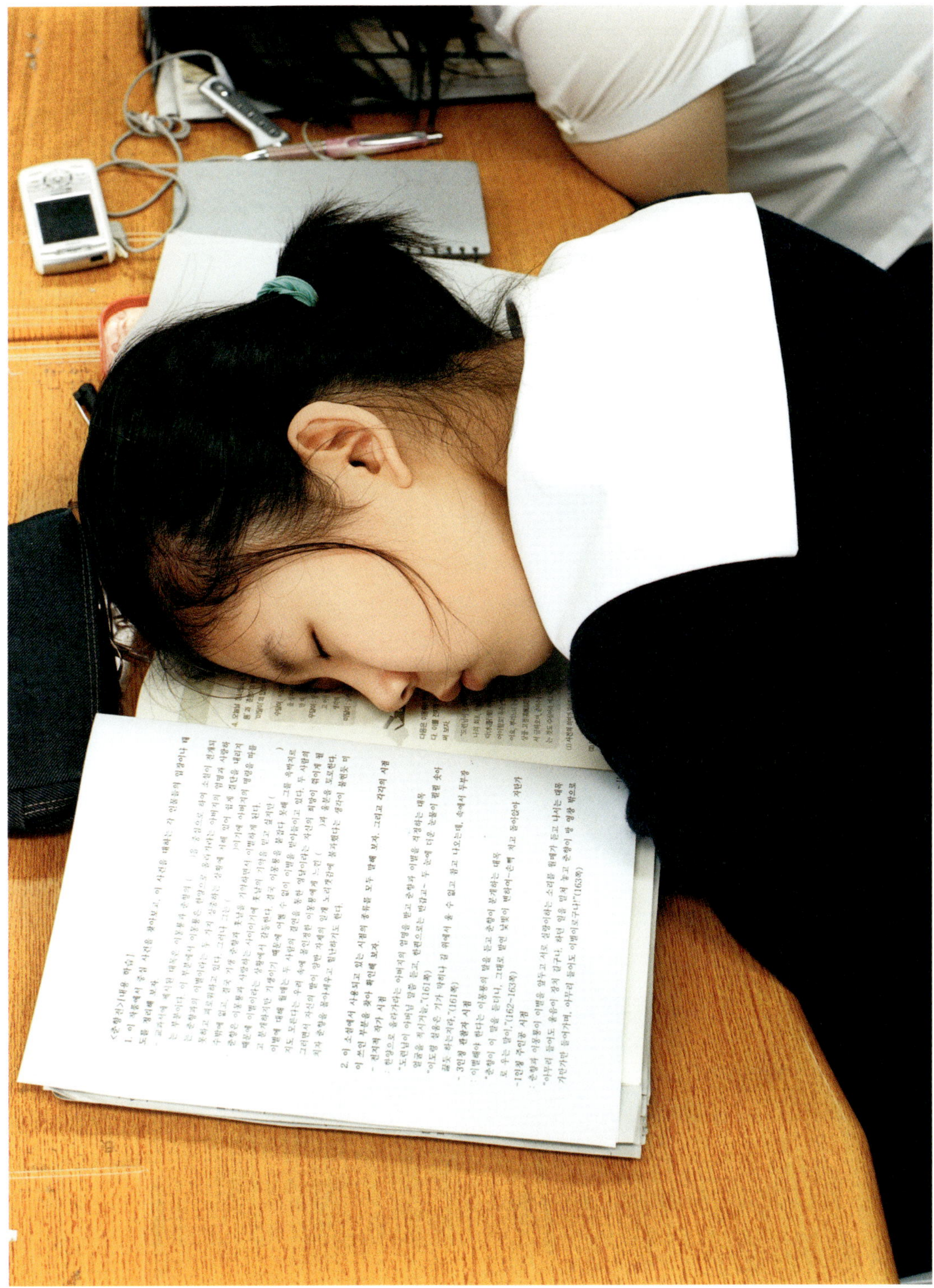

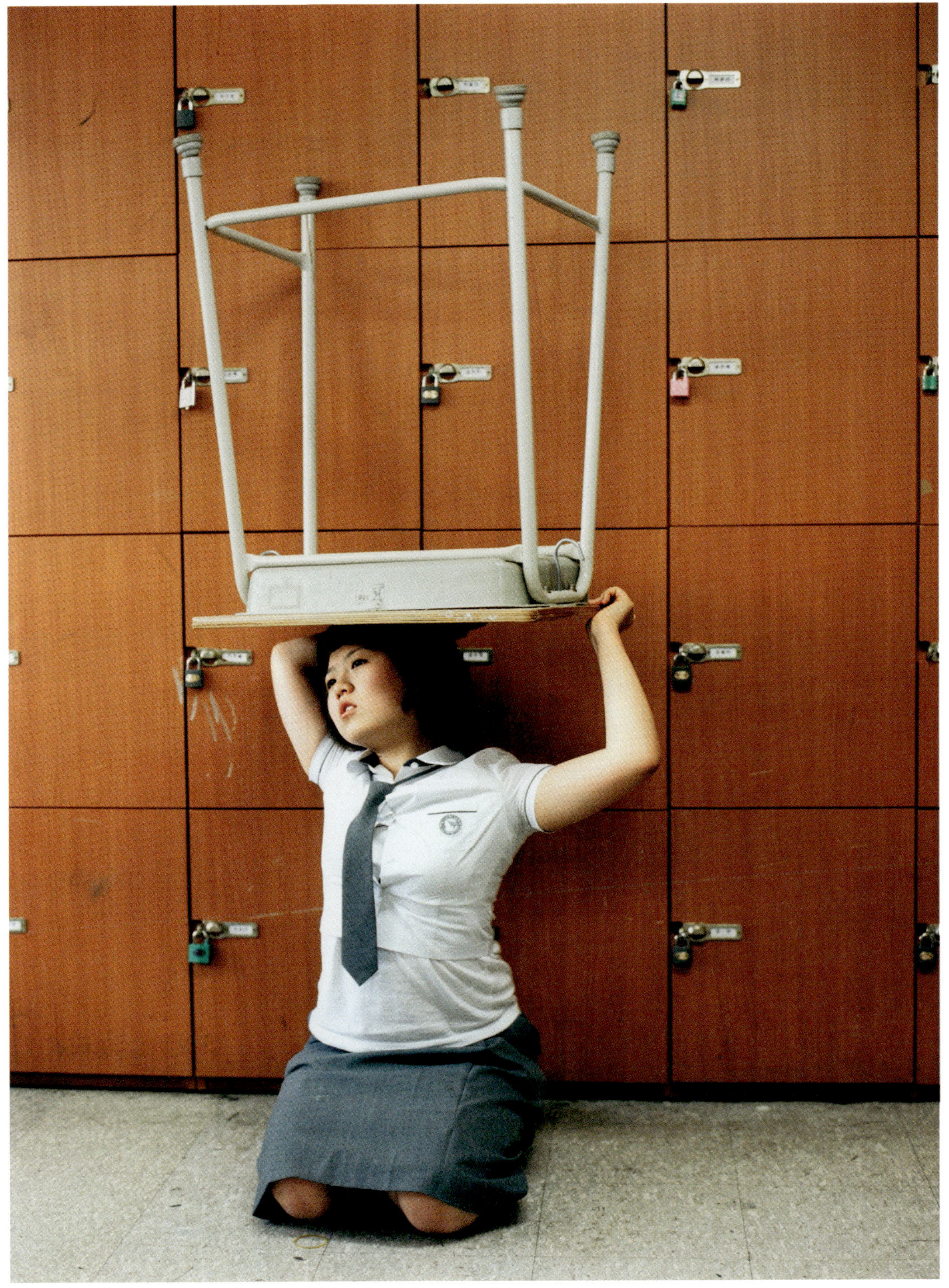

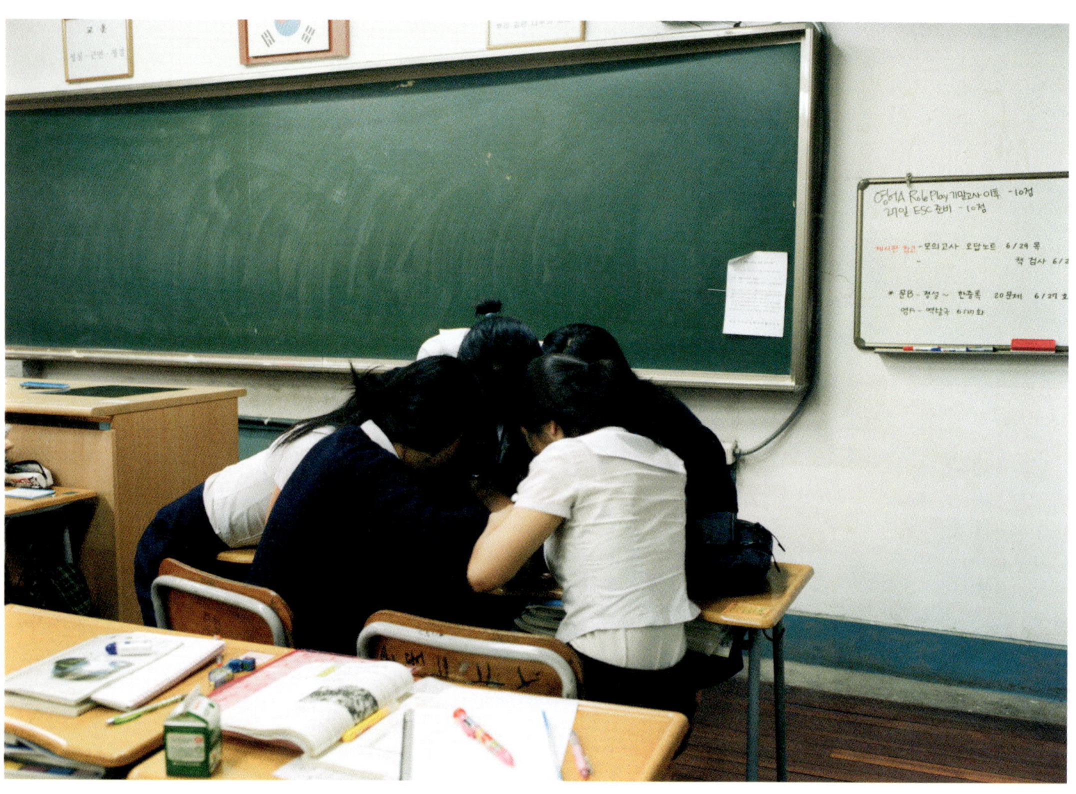

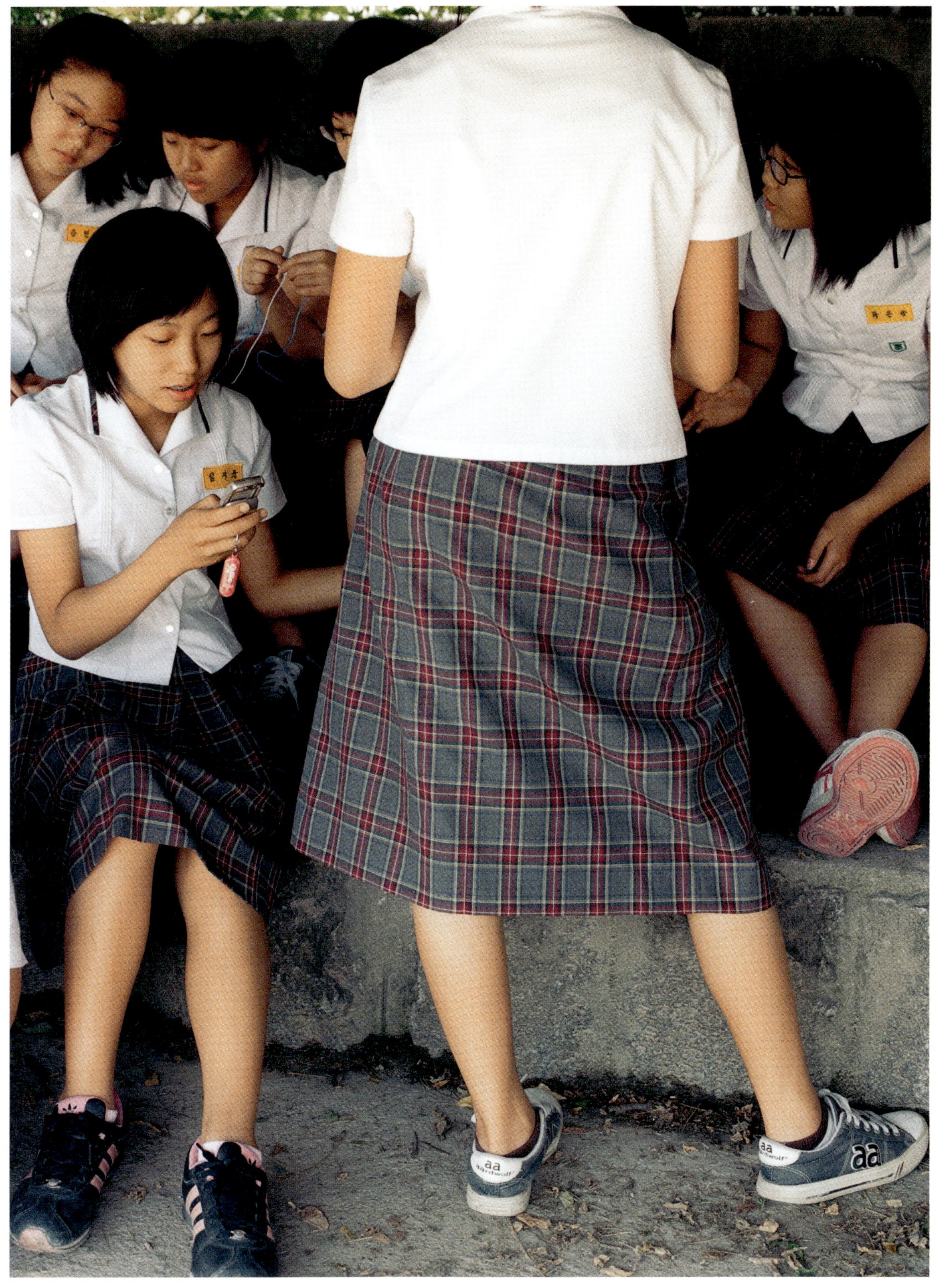

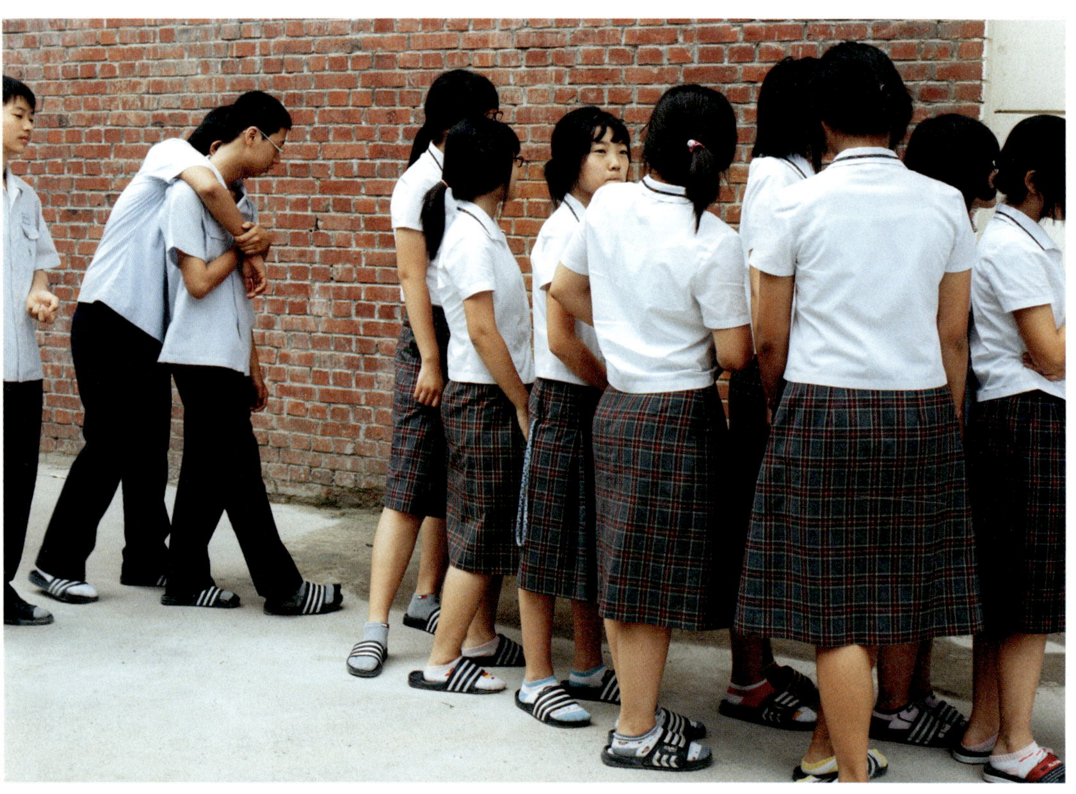

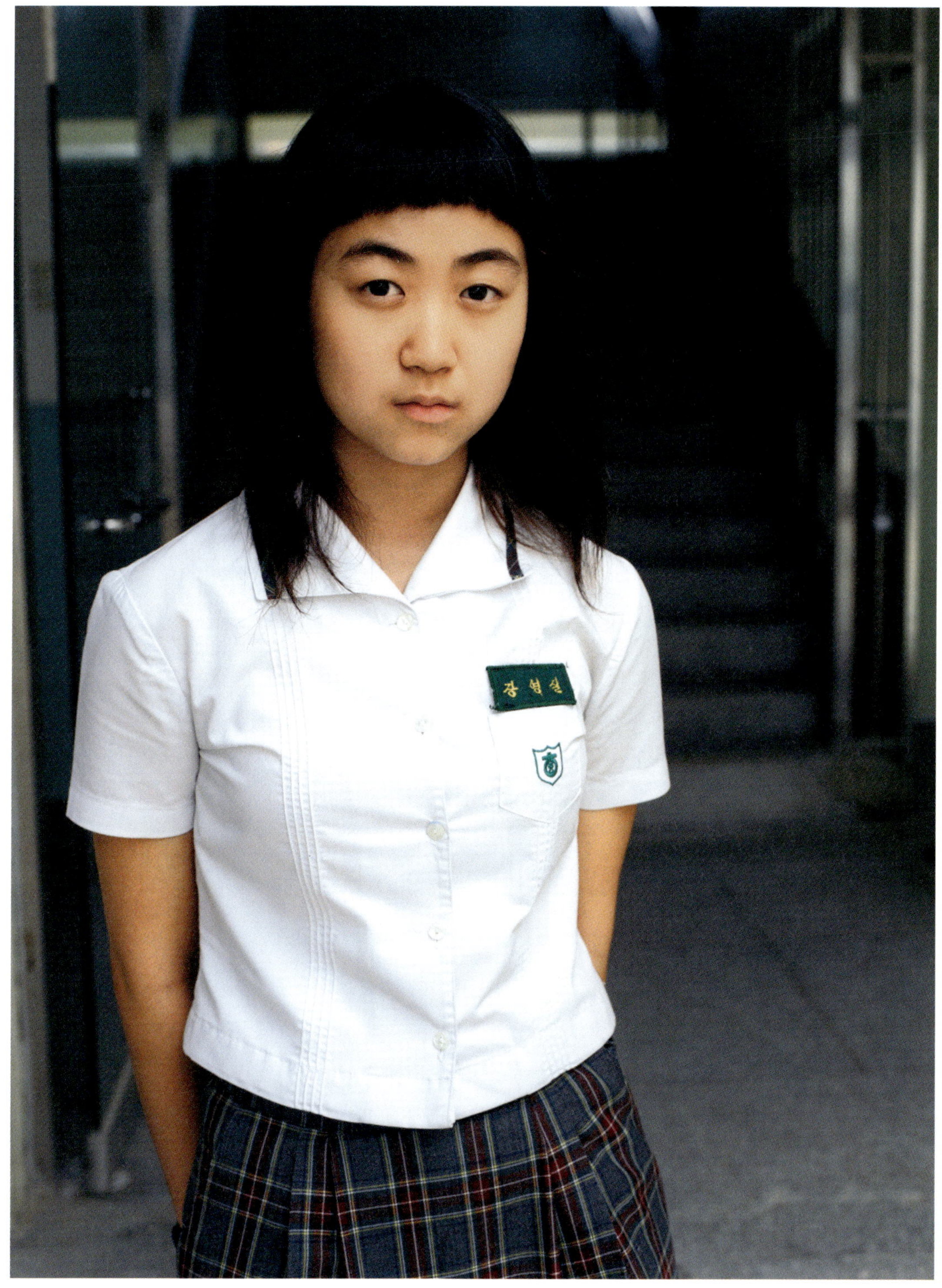

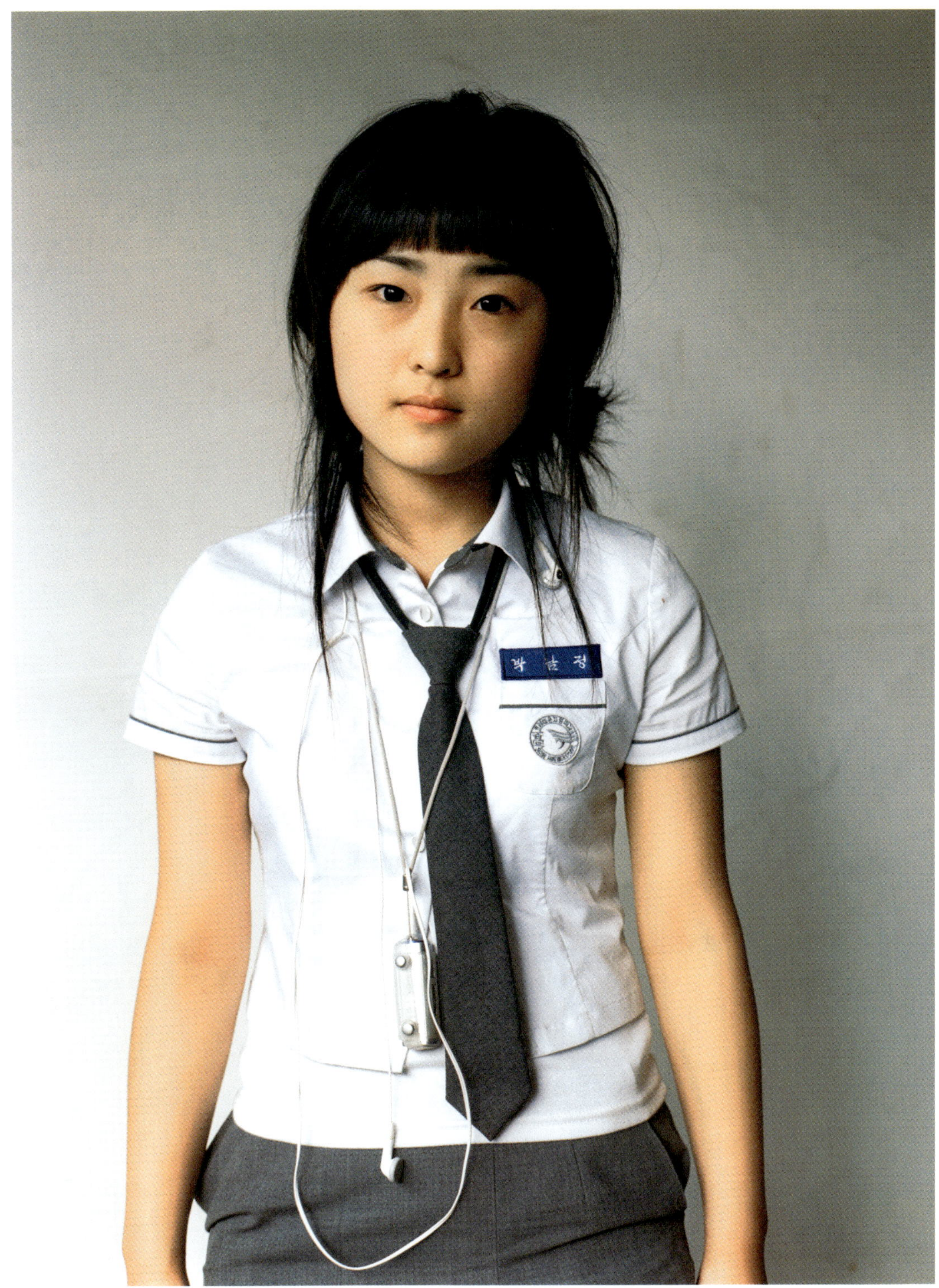

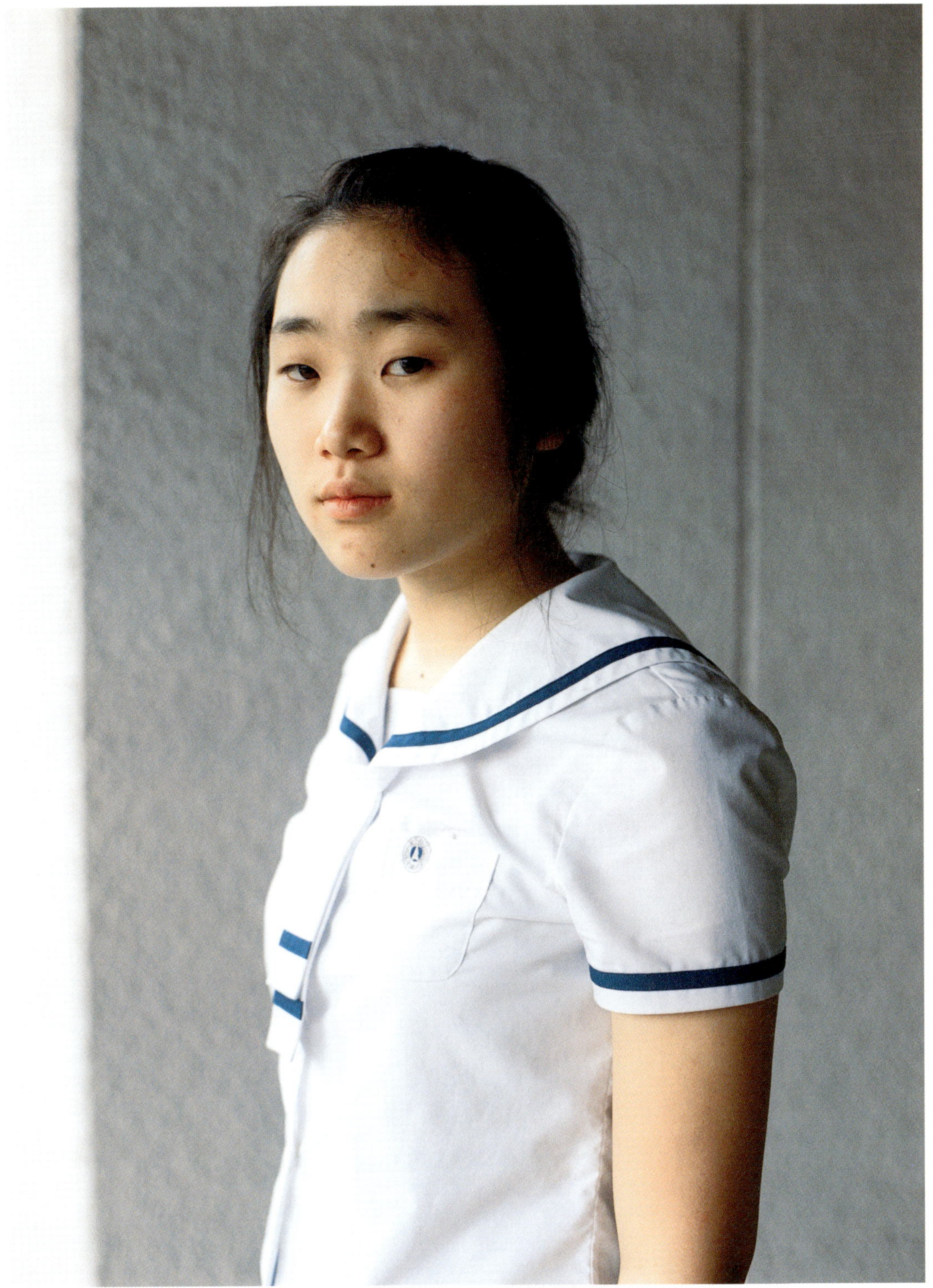

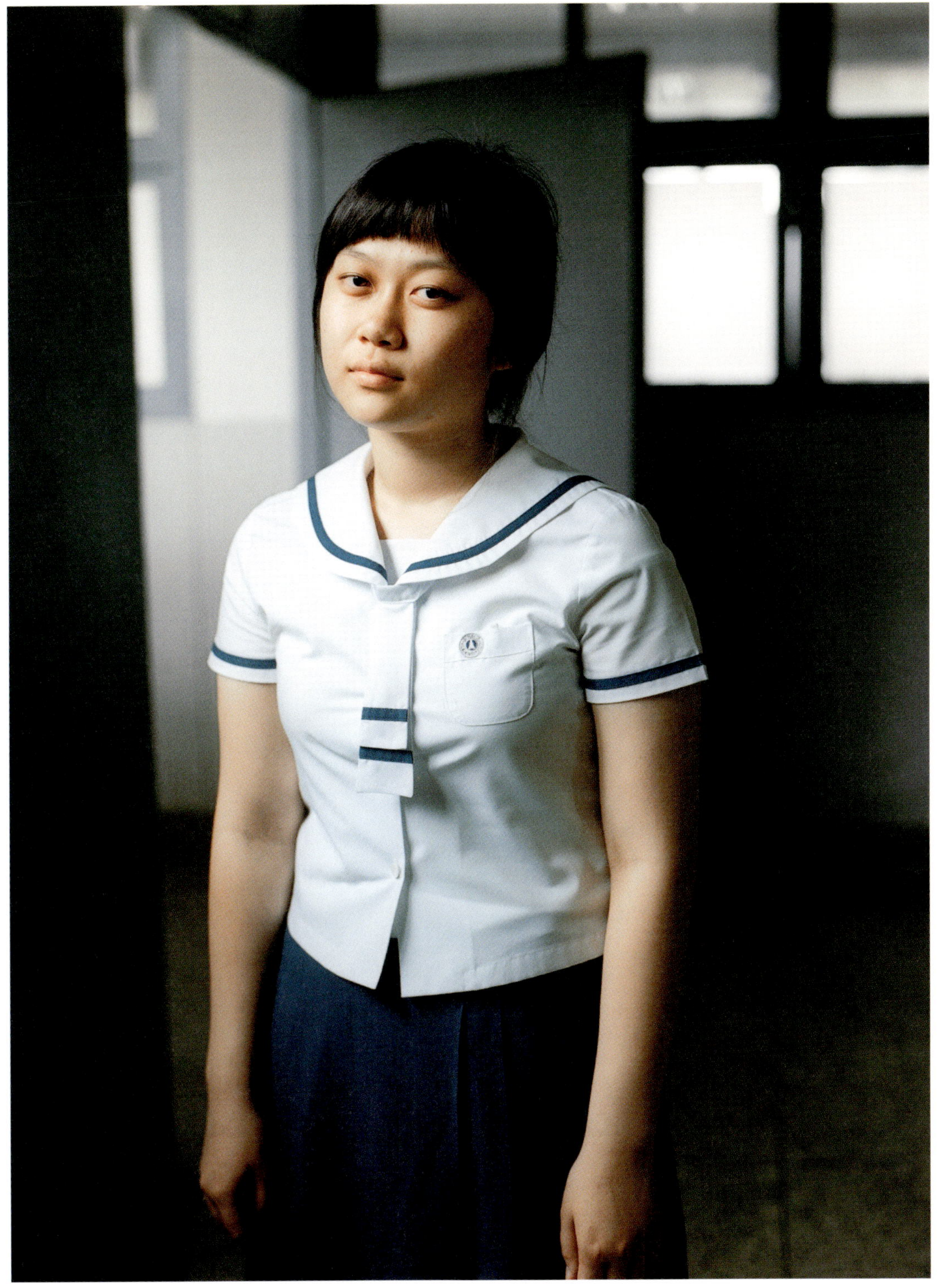

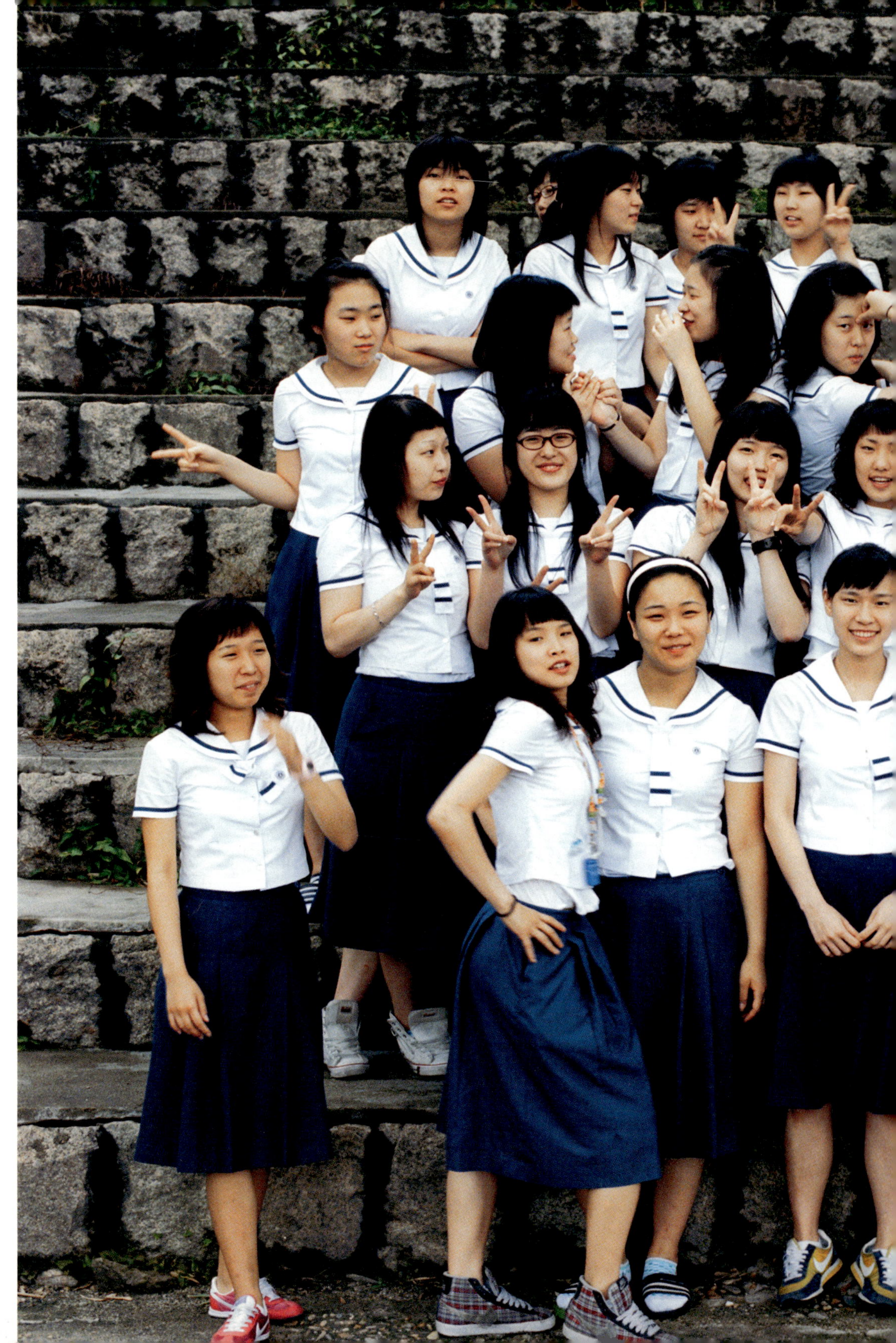

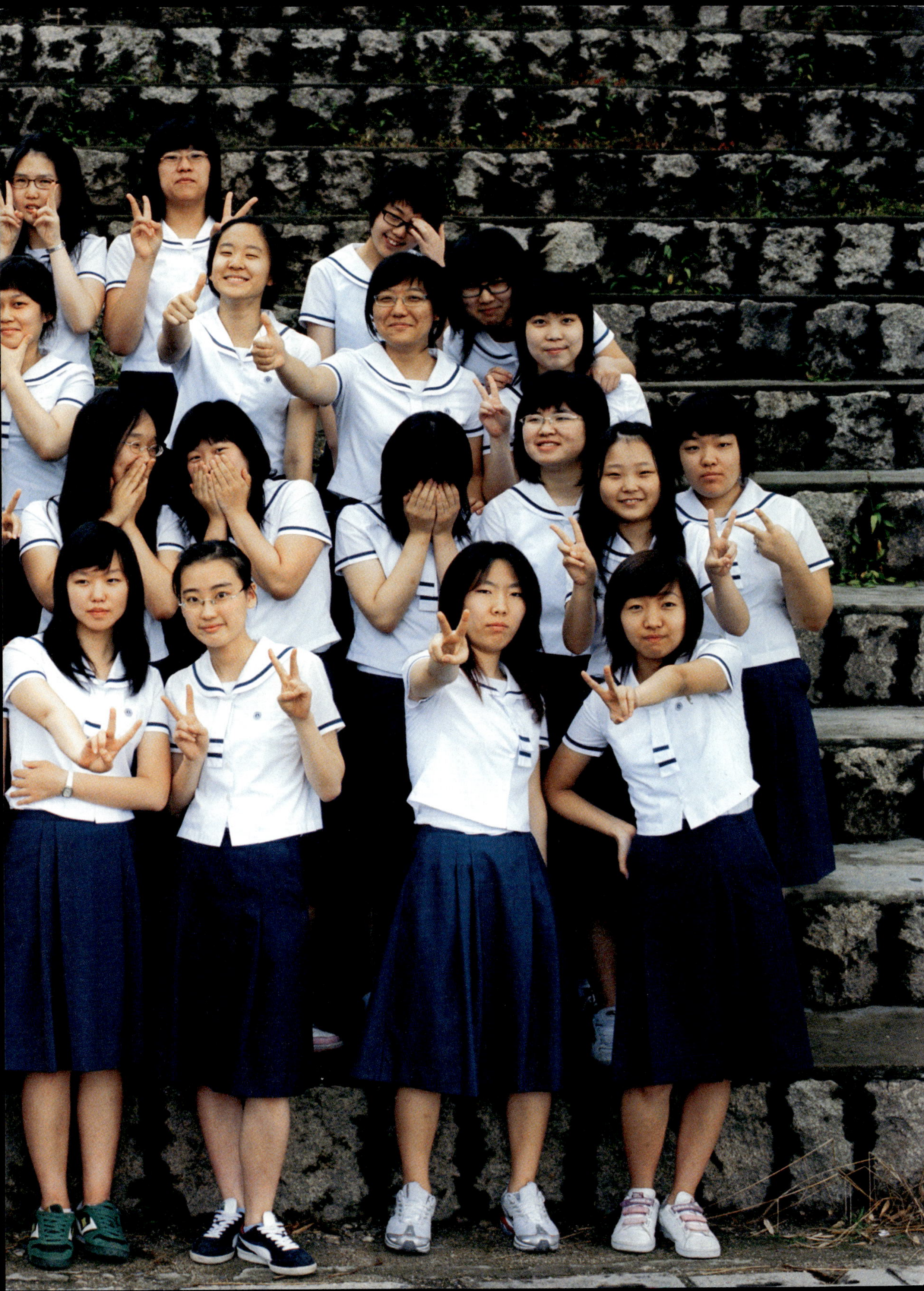

LIST OF WORKS

Chapter 1:

**Contortionist girls,
Ulaanbaatar, Mongolia 2004**

15. Portrait of a contortionist girl at the State Circus

17. Warming up at the State Circus

18. Contortionist girl in action at the State Circus

21. Odonchimeg, a contortionist girl at the State Circus

22. Odonchimeg in action at the State Circus

24. Erdenesuvd in action at the State Academic Theatre of Drama

25. Erdenesuvd at the State Academic Theatre of Drama

Chapter 2:

**Alternative youth,
Ulaanbaatar, Mongolia 2004**

29. Munconchimeg and Munkhtuya

30. Munkhtuya

31. Munkhjargal

33. Boloroo

35. Ochgerel

37. Ariunaa

38. Dulguun

39. Enkhtsetseg

40. Enerett and Tsogt

Chapter 3:

**The city of Guangzhou and
Guangdong province, China 2005**

47. A young girl after swimming,
Jing Gang

49. Two girls after swimming,
Jing Gang

50. Two girls praying, Lotus Hill
temple

51. Flowers, Guangzhou

53. A shrine at home, Jing Gang

55. Playing cards, Jing Gang

56. Selling tobacco, Jing Gang

57. Birdman in a park, Guangzhou

59. Painting, Guangzhou

61. Portrait, Guangzhou

63. Portrait, Guangzhou

65. Portrait, Guangzhou

67. Portrait, Guangzhou

68. Rapid River, Guangzhou

69. Two couples at the video
arcade, Guangzhou

71. Bus stop, Guangzhou

73. Bridge, Guanzghou

75. Umbrellas, Guangzhou

Chapter 4:

**Betel Nut Beauties,
Taiwan 2006**

79. Betel nut sign, Jhongli

81. Portrait, Hsinchu

83. Portrait of two betel nut
beauties, Hsinchu

85. Betel nut kiosk at night, Sigan

87. Portrait of two betel nut
beauties, Taipei

89. Delivering betel nuts to a
customer, Jhongli

91. Portrait, Jhongli

93. Betel nut kiosk, Miaoli

95. Betel nut kiosk, Cyonglin

97. Portrait of two betel nut beauties
and their dogs, Cyonglin

99. Portrait, Longtan

101. Preparing betel nuts, Taipei

Chapter 5:

**High Schools,
Seoul, South Korea 2006**

105. Class awards, Pung Moon Girls
High School

107. Portrait of three schoolgirls,
Hwigyong Middle School

109. Working, Pung Moon Girls
High School

111. Sleeping, Pung Moon Girls
High School

113. Punishment, Jeone Arm Beauty
High School

114. Talking, Pung Moon Girls
High School

115. In line for lunch, Hwigyong
Middle School

116. Break, Hwigyong Middle School

117. Portrait, Hwigyong Middle
School

119. Portrait, Jeone Arm Beauty
High School

121. Portrait, Seoul Girls High School

123. Portrait, Seoul Girls High School

124. An unofficial class portrait,
Seoul Girls High School

Published on the occasion of
the exhibition
Marco van Duyvendijk:
Portraits from Asia
organized by the Faulconer Gallery,
Grinnell College
6 October – 10 December 2006

Daniel Strong, Curator
Milton Severe, Exhibition Designer

© 2006 Grinnell College
Faulconer Gallery
Bucksbaum Center for the Arts
1108 Park Street
Grinnell, Iowa 50112
T. 641.269.4660
F. 641.269.4626
www.grinnell.edu/faulconergallery

ISBN-10: 0-9776779-3-1
ISBN-13: 978-0-9776779-3-1
Library of Congress Control Number:
2006937676

Faulconer Gallery staff:

Milton Severe, Director of Exhibition
Design

Daniel Strong, Associate Director and
Curator of Exhibitions

Kay Wilson, Curator of the Grinnell
College Art Collection

Lesley Wright, Director

Catalogue Design: Annabel Wimer
Design, Des Moines, Iowa

Printed in Bruges, Belgium by
Die Keure NV

Marco van Duyvendijk is represented by
Galerie Cokkie Snoei, Rotterdam
www.cokkiesnoei.com

Front cover: *Portrait*, Guangzhou,
China, 2005